AN EARLY SOVIET SAINT

KESTON BOOKS
General Editor: Michael Bourdeaux
No. 6

An Early Soviet Saint

The Life of Father Zachariah

translated by
JANE ELLIS

and with an Introduction by
SIR JOHN LAWRENCE

MOWBRAYS
LONDON & OXFORD

© 1976

ISBN 0 264 66334 9

First published 1976
by A. R. Mowbray & Co. Limited,
The Alden Press,
Osney Mead,
Oxford OX2 OEG

Photoset, printed and bound
in Great Britain by
REDWOOD BURN LIMITED
Trowbridge & Esher

92
ZIZ

78070628

Contents

Acknowledgements

The translator wishes to thank Father Michael Fortonnato, Father Sergei Hackel and Sir John Lawrence for their invaluable help with difficult points of translation.

Series Introduction

Some years ago I became aware that there were circulating in
the Soviet Union typed or manuscript copies of unpublished
books of spirituality written during the Soviet period. Of
course, these could not be printed in the Soviet Union and,
though their circulation in typescript was not strictly contrary
to Soviet law, the authorities would not view them with favour.
And Soviet law can be both hard to ascertain and remarkably
elastic, when that suits the powers that be. So the existence of
those books was not flaunted. Yet with experience of Soviet life
one learns to interpret even slight indications, and sometimes
the veil is lifted for a minute or two. What I saw convinced me
that some of these *samizdat* books were of great spiritual depth
and that a few of them would be read centuries hence. Copies of
them have now begun to arrive in the West and it is proposed to
publish them in English as a series of Modern Russian Spirituality under the general rubric of Keston Books.

They are modern in the sense that they are written in the
modern age and often written in conditions that make traditional faith very difficult. Yet they are very traditional. It
might, therefore, be thought that they appeal to a small, ageing
and diminishing group of old fashioned faithful. But the evidence shows the contrary. One should not exaggerate. In Soviet
society many are – or sometimes affect to be – indifferent to or
even hostile to religion. And there are open or secret believers,
who find it hard to get on the wavelength of traditional Russian
spirituality. Yet it is precisely among Soviet youth, and educated youth, that spirituality of this kind makes its greatest impact. Recently one of the leading laymen of the Russian
Orthodox Church, now in the West, said, 'It is only 15 per cent
of educated youth who are believers.' But those who are have

bought their faith at a price, which has made it quietly infectious. Only fifteen per cent! But these are the young men and women who are natural leaders in the new generation, and it is they who are specially drawn to writings such as these.

So the books in this series of modern Russian spirituality are also modern in the sense that they appeal to creative elements in the modern age.

SIR JOHN LAWRENCE, 1976

Introduction

I first visited Zagorsk, the monastery of St Sergius, about fifty miles from Moscow, in the late winter of 1944. The country lay deep in snow, but the sun shone brightly on the snow-touched domes and pinnacles. It was beautiful but as cold as the grave. Our footsteps were muffled by the snow and not a sound was to be heard. I was shown the empty churches and monastic buildings and, though I was not then a believer, the desolation of that cold, cold beauty entered my heart. What had happened to the monks? It was believed that one or two old men had found a lodging somewhere in the fortified walls for some years after the Soviet authorities closed the monastery, but now there was no sign of religious life.

Since then I have visited Zagorsk many times and even stayed in the monastery. Soon after my first visit the monastery and theological college were allowed to reopen and the old, warm pulsating life of central Russia's greatest holy place began again, as if it had never stopped. From early morning to dusk a continual stream of pilgrims arrives, first from the adjoining town and, as the morning goes on, from villages and small towns further down the railway line and eventually from Moscow. An unbroken round of worship goes on all day at the shrine of St Sergius. First the monks intone a special service in his honour and then the people from the surroundings arrive. When there are enough of them, I have seen a middle-aged woman tap one of the monks on the shoulder as a sign that the laity are ready to take over. The monks go away and the people go on with the singing, turning the grave Slavonic chant into a Russian folk song. There used to be an enormous book in old Slavonic characters, surely written before the Revolution, which one of the laity used to hold in the middle of the congregation. I have stood many feet behind and still have been able to read the words of the service and join in with the others. This book is no longer seen. I suppose it has at last worn out, but the pilgrims still come and there is a smaller book that they use for the same purpose. How they love St Sergius! He is not a figure from the remote fourteenth century but an ever present help in trouble, a dear friend.

The scene cannot have been very different when Father Zachariah first came to Sergievo Posad, as Zagorsk was then called. His biography is the first book in the series of books of Modern Russian Spirituality. I have not been able to ascertain much about him beyond what is in this biography, but the book speaks for itself. Father Zachariah was born in 1850, the son of peasants, and never went to school. He lived until 1936, dying at the beginning of the Great Terror. The first half of the book describes his life under Tsarism, the second under Communism. There is little mention of political events, though anyone who knows the Soviet Union can read between the lines. When the monastery was closed, Father Zachariah stayed on for some time, and no doubt some memory of him and others remained among those who told me nearly twenty years later that some of the monks had 'lived in the walls'. Eventually he was forced to move to Moscow, where the circumstances of his life are implied rather than described. He was due for arrest in the Great Terror and escaped only because he was on his death bed.

The life of this dedicated monk seems scarcely to have changed when he was forced to leave his monastery. He thanked God for 'everything', even the cruellest afflictions, whether under Tsarism or Communism, and cared for his 'spiritual children' with complete disregard for the conditions of his life. He did not hold a position of hierarchical authority in the church. He was a *starets* or elder (plural *startsy*). These *startsy* play a cardinal role in the life of the eastern Orthodox churches. They are generally simple monks whose charismatic authority is widely recognised by the believers. In the old days people from all ranks of society would cross the whole of Russia to consult a famous *starets*, or perhaps just to see him. The life of

Father Zachariah indicates some of the ways in which *startsy* worked under Soviet rule.

When Zachariah became a monk he was according to custom given a new name, Zosima. When later he entered into the highest stage of monastic life, becoming a *skhimnik*, he was required to change his name again and took his old name Zachariah. He was a medieval figure and the element of the miraculous is an integral element in his story, and could be an impediment to understanding. The stories of the *starets'* youth presumably rest on indirect evidence, and some of them have a dream-like quality which makes me, for one, disposed to 'mythologize' them. But the stories of his later years appear to rest on the direct evidence of truthful persons. Every reader will make up his own mind about them. It seems to me that there are two choices. One may say these things did not happen as they are recorded, because on *a priori* grounds one thinks they could not have happened. Or one may ask how must we conceive reality if such things are attested by credible witnesses? Personally, I consider the second choice to be the more rational. In any case, part of the interest of the story is that a figure who seems to come from a remote past should be described by twentieth-century witnesses and make such an impact on them.

Nothing is known to me about the writer of this book other than what appears from internal evidence. She was not illiterate, but she writes in a simple style that owes little to the Russian classics and much to the traditions of Slavonic spirituality, and to the way of speaking usual to those brought up in that tradition. So she brings us into a world of thought and feeling where words and ideas do not always correspond exactly with anything in the vocabulary of western Europe. This makes difficulties for the translator. How should one translate the word *prozorliv*? It indicates a penetrating gaze that may on occasion see deep into the purposes of God. Sometimes 'intuitive' seems the right translation and sometimes 'prescient'. At other times, one is at a loss for the right word.

The author of this book was the 'spiritual daughter' of Father Zachariah. This does not mean quite the same as that he was her 'director' in the western Catholic sense of the word. In the eastern Orthodox churches the relation between a 'spiritual father' and his 'spiritual sons' and 'spiritual daughters' is close. They call each other 'thou', as if they were blood relations, and there is a strong bond of affection in these elective affinities of the spiritual life. The authority of a spiritual father is enormous and is exercised by giving or withholding a blessing. To this day he may say, 'I blessed the marriage of my spiritual daughter' or 'I did not bless' a momentous journey, with the implication that the marriage took place and the journey did not. This too can lead to difficulties of translation. The same word may mean both 'to bless' and 'to permit'. Likewise, 'I do not bless' may mean, in effect, 'I forbid'.

The copy of the life of Father Zachariah which has reached the West has no title. It is typed on strong paper, but it is the bottom carbon and is hardly legible. But it is carefully bound and, on what should be the title page, there is an elaborate type-written cross.

SIR JOHN LAWRENCE

CHAPTER 1

Childhood and Vocation

The elder (*starets*) Zachariah was born on 2 September 1850. At his Baptism he was given the name Zachariah, in honour of God's prophet Zachariah, the father of John the Baptist. Zachariah's parents were peasants, the former serfs of the Naryshkin family. They lived very well and were 'masters themselves' as they used to say at that time.

They lived in the province of Kaluga. They had eleven children. Zachariah was the eleventh. Many of his brothers and sisters died after a time.

Zachariah was born not at home, but in a field. His mother Tatyana Minaevna was working until the last minute, and just before the birth of her child she went off to the field to spread flax. She went alone, and her time came, and without outside help she brought into the world a male child. It was cold. His mother laid him in her skirts, for there was nothing to wrap him in, and carried him home.

Zachariah's father, Ivan Dimitrievich, was a believing man. He often went to church and prayed diligently. He looked after his land skilfully and sometimes traded in apples and seeds, but he had a serious shortcoming: he drank a great deal, and when he was drunk he abused his wife, although he was very kind by nature. He would have a drink and say to his little son: 'Zacky, I'll bring you some presents.' 'There's no need, you're drunk,' answered his seven-year-old son, who from childhood used to turn away from everything bad and ugly. 'Oh you rogue, is that how to answer your Daddy?' his mother, Tatyana Minaevna, checked her son.

It must be said that Zachariah's mother lived a saintly life. She helped absolutely everybody and loved everybody. She gave whole loaves of bread to the poor, and meat and other

1

provisions. She did not grudge anything at all for the poor, and besides this she used to give advice. Nobody married without her advice. Tatyana Minaevna was asked about everything, and what she said was done. She enjoyed enormous respect and authority among the villagers.

In bringing up her son, she implanted in him above all a love of helping the poor and suffering as much as he could. He would be playing with the other children and feel hungry and ask for a small loaf, and his mother would give him a big loaf and say: 'First feed your friends and then eat yourself.' His saintly mother's demands were quickly implanted in the boy's tender heart.

When Zachariah's father went out to trade his seeds and apples he would take his son with him, but no sooner did he move away than the little boy would begin giving away his wares free to the poor. He would call to the customers and share out his wares with them with a generous hand.

Children loved the gentle Zachariah and nicknamed him 'the priest'. 'We'll build a church in the field and you, Zacky, will be our priest and marry us,' his young friends used to say.

His mother worshipped her son, but as soon as he had grown a little, when he was seven, he began to run away from his home into the fields and the woods and disappear there for several days. His mother would fall asleep and he would get up at night as quiet as a mouse, and was gone before anyone saw him. He would go somewhere a short distance away and climb into a tall fir tree, put his arms round its trunk and sit in solitude, praying and thinking about the things of God. He would spend an entire night without sleep, not climbing down from his refuge. He knew that what he was doing was drawing him to solitude, to spiritual feats. All these days he ate nothing except roots from the grass, and his childish heart overflowed with holy joy and zeal for God.

When day began to break he would come down from the fir tree for a little while, but as soon as he caught sight of any passer-by he would climb back up into it again.

His mother, of course, was very worried when she saw her beloved son disappearing like this for days on end; she looked for him everywhere, weeping and sorrowing. Finally she decided to go to the local priest to talk to him and ask for advice in her grief.

The village priest, who was in retirement, was a hundred years old: a good, gracious man, he healed the sick and drove out demons. For his humility, God had given Father Alexei grace and prescience.

Tatyana Minaevna came to him with her little son and said, weeping: 'Father Alexei, I have one son left, I have buried five, but this little chick will not survive either, he runs away from home and hides for whole days in the forest . . . .'

Father Alexei prayed and God revealed Zachariah's future to him. He said to his mother: 'Don't weep, your son will bring you joy, but he won't be a breadwinner; he will be a monk and will live to a ripe old age.'

When Zachariah was sixteen years old he was sent off to the town to work making bast matting; he had no schooling at all. Soon after his departure his mother took to her bed.

Sensing that her end was near, she blessed everyone and said to her daughter: 'Maria, I have said goodbye to everyone, there is only my dear Zachariah that I have not managed to bless; when I have blessed my son, then I will die. I shall ask God for a delay, and you go and fetch him.' They went for Zachariah and brought him back late in the evening. His sister called him to the dying woman. 'Mummy, do you know who has come?' Her son burst into tears.

This is how the elder recounts his farewell to his dying mother. In the morning Maria and Anisya went off to the village. 'Sit down with me, it is only you that I feel sorry for,' said his mother. 'My dear Zachariah, listen, these are the temptations that will face you: matches with many brides will be made for you, but you will not marry; there will be brides for you from our village and from others . . .' and she named them all. 'Remember that if you enter a monastery I will rejoice, but your father will coerce you into family life. Don't listen to him. Father Alexei said that you would be a monk.'

Then his mother took an icon of Our Lady of Kazan which she had bought when Zachariah was eight years old. 'Here is your Guide,' she said to him, pointing to the icon of the Mother of God. Then she ordered that her daughters, who had returned, should light the stove, give her beloved son a good square meal and take him back into the town. 'Don't cry, Zachariah darling,' his mother consoled him, 'don't cry, I don't want your dear eyes to suffer, I don't want your lovely blue eyes to be reddened. Go away and don't come back soon. Your father will come to call you back, but stay there all the same and work; when I am being buried retreat into yourself and pray inwardly, but don't come to my grave.'

And so according to his mother's words he said farewell and went away.

At the very moment when Tatyana Minaevna passed away, Zachariah felt as if a wonderful fragrance of incense was enveloping him: 'My mother has died,' he said, and burst into tears. Next morning people came to him and told him how quietly and peacefully his mother had died. She did not want to see any demons and said to her daughter: 'Pray and stand near me, otherwise I'll be afraid of demons; I've detained you on account of Zachariah, otherwise I would have died earlier.' But her daughter was rather afraid and went away. Then the mother half-rose, made the sign of the cross over her pillow, crossed herself and gave up her soul.

Later, when Zachariah became an elder, he used to tell how, when talking to a demon, he asked him: 'Do you have any Christians in hell?' 'Of course,' replied the demon, 'your father was there, but you took him away by the alms which you gave for his soul and by prayer.' 'And my mother?' 'Your mother was not there, she scattered her whole path with pieces of bread and we did not see where she went past, although we looked very hard.'

Tatyana Minaevna died on 31 October. The elder Zachariah often said: 'Whoever remembers my parents Tatyana and Ioann after their burial, the Lord himself will remember him.'

On the fortieth day Zachariah hurried home as fast as he could. He had no warm clothing and he set off on his journey quite inadequately dressed. He had to go nearly five miles, there was a fierce frost of thirty or so degrees Centigrade and a strong wind. The young traveller slept for three or four hours. Suddenly he heard a wonderful, authoritative voice – it was his Guardian Angel awaking him. 'Arise, it is time to go.' This was repeated several times, until Zachariah awoke and realised the danger of his position.

He got up and set off, and he became as warm as if someone were warming him, or as if summer had come.

Yes, it was a miracle of the grace of God that Zachariah did not freeze during his lengthy sleep in such severe frost.

After his mother's death, as she had foretold, temptations rained down upon Zachariah. People began to suggest brides for him, but he kept refusing. Zachariah kept clear of marriage by every possible means. Finally, on his father's instructions, Zachariah was taken to another place to look at a bride. An old man came to fetch him and took him seventeen miles away from his own home. 'Ah,' he said, 'my grand-daughter is so good, wouldn't you like to marry her?' Zachariah muffled himself up in his fur coat and made no reply. At length they drew up at the gates. 'Open the gates,' shouted the old man. 'Who's there, is it you, grandfather?' 'Yes, it's me, I've brought you a bridegroom, come and have a look at him.' But when she heard this she ran away.

Supper was served and the bride came and sat beside her father, but she had covered her face with a shawl. After supper she began to take off her father's boots, and Zachariah said: 'I don't want to get married, and why doesn't she show her face, she's covered it up, completely covered it. Surely I haven't come to look at a shawl?' On the next day the bride's mother cooked pancakes and prepared dinner in the best room. At dinner Anastasya Maximovna took off her shawl and was covered in blushes and Zachariah was immediately attracted to her. For a few minutes they were left alone together. 'Will you marry me?', said Zachariah. 'Yes,' she replied.

But matters became so complicated that for a year and a half Zachariah was not able to marry, and he began to dream that his bride appeared to him, looking very elegant, and seeming to say to her fiancé: 'Why don't you get married?' He replied: 'I will get married, I will. Just be careful that they don't marry you off to someone else.'

As a result of all these experiences and meditations Zachariah grew very thin. Once he arrived during a fast at his sister's house, and she said to him: 'Why, you've made yourself quite weak by fasting, you've become terribly thin!' Her brother replied: 'I am twenty years old, it must be time for me to marry. I'm preparing myself, and I eat once a day. My father insists that I should marry soon. For three years I have been asking my father to let me go to a monastery, but he will not agree, and now I keep dreaming about my bride, so I'm going to get married.'

Zachariah's sister Maria was a married woman much older than him. The Lord inspired her to say this: 'You must go by a different way, brother, all this is the enemy's influence over you. Tonight, Zacky, your fate will be decided. When you go to bed, make a large sign of the cross over your bed at the head and the feet, above and below, and also at the sides. Then you will see what happens.'

Zachariah did this and went to sleep peacefully. Towards morning he had a dream: a woman dressed in a gown as white as snow came into his room, made three low bows to the icons and, turning to him, said: 'Zachariah, how could you take it into your head to marry? No, you will not marry, you will be a monk. Remember, your mother gave you her blessing to go to Three Streams Monastery at White Shores, so go on; your father has not allowed you to go so far, but now he will let you.'

Zachariah immediately recognised the Protectress of the Christian family, the Most Pure and Ever Virgin Mother of God. A feeling of lightness, calmness and joy came over his soul. It was as if some inward disease had passed away and complete healing had come.

On the morning of St Lazarus's Day* he addressed his father: 'Let me go to White Shores, to the Mother of God at Three Streams. Mother made a vow and did not have time to fulfil it. I have decided to fulfil it for her.' Zachariah resorted to guile. His father believed him and said: 'Well, why not, go on

* St Lazarus's Day is observed on Passion Sunday, the week before Palm Sunday. (Translator's note.)

then, there is nothing to do now, during the fast, but later when you return, then you will marry.'

Zachariah took with him the icon of Our Lady of Kazan which his mother had given him with her blessing, wrapped it up in a towel and put it into a bag. Turning to his father, he said: 'You bless me too, father.'

'You have your mother's blessing.' 'No, you bless your children too.' His father took the icon of the Resurrection of Christ to bless his son. He blessed him and then suddenly began to sob and fell to the floor. Zachariah caught the icon to stop it falling. His father turned to him and said: 'I feel that you are abandoning me completely.'

Zachariah felt wretched, and he was sorry for his father. He hastily said farewell, saying: 'Let your blessing remain at home for the time being. I am going only as far as Three Streams.' He said farewell and started running through unknown fields and woods quickly, as quickly as he could. Zachariah was afraid his father would change his mind and pursue him.

Then, at last, still with the icon of Our Lady of Kazan, he arrived at the White Shores monastery. He began to beg the superiors to accept him as one of the brothers, but nothing of the sort, they kept on refusing him.

Once, on the fifteenth of June, Zachariah pleaded almost in tears to be allowed to remain. Finally they accepted him temporarily and gave him the duty* of herding the calves. But before he set about this duty, the abbot sent him home for his documents. Moreover, he ordered him to go down to Optina Monastery.† 'I,' he said, 'do not have the gift of prescience, but go to Father Ambrose, and do whatever he says.'

Zachariah was very afraid of going to Optina Monastery. One thought troubled him: suppose he did not receive a blessing there to become a monk? But if he was sent, he must go. Obedience is disobedience to the devil.

* The word which we have translated as 'duty', *poslushaniye*, means more exactly a task performed by a monk in obedience to his superiors. (Translator's note.)

† Optina Pustyn was a famous monastery at Kozelsk near Moscow, where throughout the nineteenth century there was a series of *startsy* whose counsel was sought by pilgrims and visitors from all over Russia. (Translator's note.)

Zachariah took his bag and set off. His way lay through a forest. He saw standing there a small wooden chapel, and near it was a majestic woman deep in profound prayer, with upraised arms, as the Mother of God is portrayed in her icon 'The Sign'. Zachariah hid behind a tree so as not to disturb her and began to wait.

At last she finished praying. She glanced around, saw Zachariah and said: 'Weren't you with us in the monastery at Three Streams? They'll take you into the cloister, won't they? After so many applications they'll take you. And now you're going to fetch your documents? First, however, follow me.' Zachariah submitted at once to the words of the unknown woman and followed her. As they walked along she said to him firmly and with authority: 'Go down to Optina, stay with Father Ambrose and let him bless you. But before you go to him, stop at the grave of the elder Macarius and pray for him. Make twelve bows to him and say: "Give rest with the saints, O Lord, to the elder and archimandrite-*skhimnik** Macarius." He was a saintly man.'

They talked together and walked farther and farther. She led Zachariah in quite a different direction from the one he had been taking. 'I had a one and only son,' she said, 'but wicked people took him from me and killed him.'

Thus they walked two miles without noticing. The woman halted and said: 'Now I am going into this village; I wish you a safe journey. Visit the grave of the elder Macarius and talk to the elder Ambrose and he will give you his blessing to enter the monastery.' Saying this, the mysterious woman vanished. Astonished by her disappearance, Zachariah looked right, left, upwards – where could she be? She was nowhere to be found. 'O Lord, who is this woman?' He began to think and to recall her conversation and suddenly he understood everything. 'Of course, she is the Mother of God!' He cheered up. ' "Praise to Thee, O Lord." But where have I come to? I go on and on . . . I don't know where I am . . .' He came to a river. But there was no thought of crossing the river; it was too deep and wide.

---

* A *skhimnik* (plural *skhimniki*) is one who has achieved the *skhima*, the highest level of Russian monasticism, often reached only when the monk is on his death-bed. (Translator's note.)

There was no bridge anywhere. Surely he could not swim across? 'No, I can't do that – it's April.* O Lord my God, where have you brought me, O Queen of Heaven, what am I to do now?'

So Zachariah's thoughts ran. Suddenly he saw two peasants on a pair of horses riding across the river. It was so deep that at times even the horses' heads were completely covered by the water. 'Oh, what shall I do? Our Lady, help me. How am I to get across this river?' Zachariah asked the peasants. 'Go farther to the right, there's a white path there on the right, go along that.' Zachariah obeyed and went to the right, holding his mother's icon and pressing himself to the Mother of God with love in his heart. His lips moved in prayer. Looking round he saw that there really was a white path, apparently made of stone, stretching across the river. Crossing himself, he set off along it and crossed safely to the other bank. When he had crossed he asked: 'Which is the way to Optina?' He was told: 'It's late now, go to the right, to the parish priest, he is a good man and will let you stay the night.'

Zachariah set off, arrived at the priest's house and asked: 'May I stay the night? I am going from White Shores to Optina.' 'But how did you cross the river here?' 'Like this; two peasants pointed out to me a white path across the river and I crossed by that. They were riding on horses, they waded into the river and I noticed them and asked them the way. It was already twilight, but I quickly found the white path across the river and crossed by it.'

The priest sighed and said: 'First let us go into the church and pray.' He opened the church and led Zachariah into it.

It turned out that there was no such white path across the river and also that people could not have ridden across on horses in such deep water. They had not been peasants, but two angels of the Lord. Wonderful are Thy ways, O Lord.

The next day Zachariah reached Optina monastery. First of all, as he had been told, he set out for the grave of the elder Macarius, but he could not find it anywhere. Whom should he ask? Suddenly a boy of about twelve ran out of the Holy Gates

* In April the stream would have been in spate. (Translator's note.)

and said: 'Let me take you to the grave of the elder Macarius.' Zachariah followed him.

The boy led him up to the elder's grave and said: 'Well, let us make twelve bows and at every bow say: "Give rest, O Lord, to the soul of your deceased servant the elder Macarius, give rest to him with the saints."'

This they did, and then the boy vanished. How did he disappear, where did he go, who was he?

Zachariah questioned the monks about the boy, and they told him that there had never been any such boy among them. Later Zachariah realised that here also the mercy of God had been shown to him.

Zachariah liked everything at Optina: the holy tranquillity, the spirit of prayer, which seemed to pass over into nature and intensify and clarify it.

Zachariah stayed in the monastery hostel, where he could remain for a limited number of days. Every day he tried to get to the great elder Ambrose, but he had no success at all. Great crowds of people clustered around the elder Ambrose's cell, and there was no possibility of his receiving them all.

Zachariah rigorously attended all the church services, and also visited the cell of the prescient elder Ilarion. As he approached his cell, he was repeating to himself quite inaudibly the Jesus Prayer.* 'Amen,' the elder replied through the closed door. The door was opened and he received Zachariah joyfully and affectionately.

Zachariah bowed three times to the icons and the elder, who did not know him at all and had no conception of his life and his plans, said to him: 'So your mother has died? Mind you don't marry now, and your father will let you go to the monastery.'

Zachariah also visited the abbot Isaac; he visited everyone it was possible to visit.

The last day of his stay in the hostel arrived, and he felt sorrowful because he would have to leave Optina without seeing Father Ambrose. Zachariah stood through the early and late

---

* A prayer which many Orthodox repeat constantly, the full text of which is: 'O Lord, Jesus Christ, Son of God, have mercy on me, a sinner.' (Translator's note.)

liturgies, praying fervently. The monks noticed him, called him into the refectory and gave him food and drink, but his sadness did not pass away.

Returning to the hostel he took his bag to pack it and depart, but first he took out of it the icon of Our Lady of Kazan, his mother's bequest. He looked at the most pure face of the Ever Virgin Mary and burst into tears, saying: 'Mother of God, was it not you who accompanied me, was it not you who told me that I would visit Father Ambrose, and yet I am departing and I have not seen him.' Burning tears flooded the icon and fell onto the ground like rain.

Suddenly the Mother of God came to life and stepped out of the icon, like a maiden of indescribable beauty, looked at Zachariah and said: 'Follow me'. She set off so quickly that Zachariah could scarcely catch up with her. On the way he met Father Pimen. This elder lived a very strict life and allowed no-one to approach him. The Mother of God pointed her hand to Zachariah and said: 'Pimen, give him your blessing.' He blessed him at once. At last they went out behind a fence. It was clear that the Mother of God was leading Zachariah to Father Ambrose. There were the holy gates. The Mother of God halted and announced: 'Women are not allowed to enter here, but you go now to Father Ambrose, he will receive you.' And the holy Guide vanished.

Zachariah felt encouraged and went boldly toward the hut in which the elder lived.

Father Ambrose came out to the doorway himself and called Zachariah in. He received him as though he had been waiting for him for a long time. He led him into a separate room, sat him on a small divan and had a nice, affectionate, heart-to-heart talk with him. The whole of the young novice's life was an open book to the elder. Before Zachariah could open his mouth, Father Ambrose had already begun to speak: 'Well, now, my dear, so your mother has died? Listen to me, abandon your bride, do not marry, but enter the monastery. Don't think about your father now, he will let you go himself, he will not hinder you in your intention of becoming a monk. You did well in coming here. You see that on my wall are written down your

four sins. Repent of them, go down to White Shores and prepare there by fasting. Remember that in the Kingdom of
Heaven a green oak has been planted for you.'

This truly great elder spoke with Zachariah of much more
that was edifying and good for the soul. Then he blessed him
and let him go. Zachariah picked up his bag and set off on his
return journey.

'First I will call in at White Shores,' he thought, 'and prepare
there by fasting, as Father Ambrose instructed. Indeed I do
have four sins on my conscience; how did he guess them? Then
I'll go to my father for my documents and return to the monastery to take up permanent residence there.'

After his arrival at White Shores he fasted and almost at once
fell ill, so gravely that he was sent to the hospital in Bryansk.
His father was informed that his son was near to death. He
came to Bryansk and was startled by Zachariah's state of
health. Every day the old man went to church to pray for his
Zachariah, but nonetheless his son did not recover; all the time
the young novice grew worse and worse. Three months had
already passed by and he was still between life and death. He
would not take the medicines he was offered, but only prayed
diligently to the Mother of God. At last the doctors refused to
treat him and wrote to White Shores: 'Your monk has already
been lying here for three months, and this is no almshouse, but
he refuses to be treated, and only says: "I don't believe in your
medicines, the Mother of God will come and heal me," – what
kind of talk is this, what kind of capriciousness? He is so ill that
he will certainly die, but with his character we cannot help him,
so we beg you to take your monk back.'

The following answer arrived from White Shores: 'We have
no need of such a novice, we are banishing him from the monastery.'

Then Zachariah besought the Mother of God: 'Queen of
Heaven, you alone are my Protectress, help me, heal me . . .'

Then he had a dream. The Most Pure and Ever Virgin Mary
came to him, touched his head with her hand and said: 'You
will live, you will be a monk, you will live with me.' The Virgin
began to leave him. Before her a fence opened, she went

through into a wonderful garden and the fence closed once more.

Suddenly Zachariah felt a strong desire to go, to follow, to fly after her. But how? He could not go through the wall. 'Oh, I would like to be a sparrow and fly after her,' and in an instant he turned into a bee and flew in her wake . . . Next Zachariah saw in his dream that he had reached the fence in the form of a sparrow and there in the garden he saw the Mother of God in her wonderful beauty and the Saviour himself as a little boy and a throng of angels, girded with many-coloured, criss-crossing ribbons. He heard a voice: 'No-one may enter here unless Our Lady will receive him.' The angels were all in wonderful, coloured, heavenly clothes and were all planting trees. Suddenly Zachariah heard the voice of the Queen of Heaven: 'Plant a tree in his name too.' As soon as Our Lady had pronounced these words, the angels said among themselves: 'He is accepted among us.' Zachariah was unspeakably overjoyed and fell off the fence straight into the garden in the form of a sparrow, and there he stayed.

This remarkable dream produced a wonderfully powerful effect on the young, ailing novice. He fell into deep thought. Towards morning he had another dream. The abbot Israel, who had accepted him at White Shores and afterwards died, seemed to come to him and say: 'You have spent long enough in bed, get up.'

In the morning, to everyone's surprise, he woke up completely well. In the town he had a drink of tea for the first time during his entire illness, and went off to White Shores. He had a very unfriendly reception there, but all the same they let him stay. In all he lived there for one year, from 1870 to 1871.

On this occasion, having returned from Bryansk, Zachariah felt weak, and his health was not properly restored. All the same he went through his duties: he watched over the calves, painted buildings, covered the church roofs with paint. The abbot in the monastery then was Father Joseph, who tried by every means to send him home, but Zachariah did not give way and begged him to be allowed to stay there.

Abbot Israel appeared to him in a dream a second time and

said: 'Do not oppose the abbot, go home with your father.'
Zachariah obeyed. Having gone back to his native haunts with
his father, he took to his bed again and lay there for another two
months, taking no food at all. He asked his father to boil him
some hay and drank this broth.

When Zachariah had recovered slightly, his father advised
him to live in the forest for a while with a hermit, the elder
Daniel, who had lived for forty years in an isolated spot in the
Kaluga region. 'You will be a cell-servant for the elder Daniel,'
said his father, 'and I will supply provisions for you there.'

Now his father seemed to understand his son's vocation to
monkhood and had nothing against his ascetic life. In fact he
wanted him to live in the forest with the elder as a form of relax-
ation and for his health to recover before he entered the monastery.

Zachariah moved in with the elder, who received him wil-
lingly. He lived with him for several months, until the week of
'The Women Myrrh-Bearers'.* The elder Daniel was a zealot
who observed the fasts. He ate nothing during the whole of the
Great Lent Fast, and only at the Annunciation and on Palm
Sunday did he fortify himself with some meagre food.

Father Daniel greatly revered the elder Melchizedek, who
lived to be 110 years old (his life is described in the book *Spiritual
Leaders of Piety†* of the eighteenth to nineteenth centuries). He
carried on the ascetic work of Melchizedek in the forest in the
place where he had lived, and it was as though he were linked
with him in his soul. In the elder Daniel's cell hung Father
Melchizedek's monk's cloak.

Zachariah had a good life with the elder and studied a truly
Christian monastic life in practice.

The elder often began to remind Zachariah that quite soon
he must depart for White Shores to his former novitiate. But

---

* The third Sunday in Easter. These are the women who brought the spices
to the Lord's tomb for his burial. (Translator's note.)

† This phrase gives the approximate meaning of the virtually untranslata-
ble '*Podvizhniki Blagochestiya*'. A *podvizhnik*, for which we have used throughout
the term 'spiritual leader' is a monk or hermit who conducts a life of great
effort towards inner conformity with Christ, and on whom people look as an
example. (Translator's note.)

then Zachariah became so gravely ill that he made a vow to make his home with St Sergius at the Holy Trinity Monastery.

'I have heard,' Zachariah said at that time, 'that you have bad monks, Father Sergius, but I am worse than all the very worst and most wicked monks, so accept me into the number of your brothers. I want to live with you, Venerable Father, and I give this vow.' Immediately the saint raised him up from his grave illness.

Zachariah felt sad that the elder was sending him to White Shores, as he wanted to fulfil his vow, but he could not make up his mind to mention it.

One day Zachariah had a wonderful dream. He seemed to see the elder Melchizedek coming to him, kissing him three times and saying: 'Where is it you are going to and leaving me?' Zachariah replied: 'The elder Daniel is sending me away to White Shores.' 'Call him to me,' said Melchizedek. Zachariah ran to fetch the elder. When the elders saw each other, Melchizedek said: 'Christ is among us,' and kissed him three times. 'Do not send him to White Shores, let him go to St Sergius,' he said, pointing to Zachariah. 'And now prepare me something to eat.'

Suddenly Zachariah's sister appeared and began to prepare a meal. Between Melchizedek and Daniel stood a radiant angel, very beautiful, and said to Melchizedek: 'Lead Zachariah to St Sergius.'

Immediately Zachariah felt himself rising up into the air and flying away. There were the golden cupolas of the Moscow churches, shops and even signboards. Zachariah and the angel flew without stopping right up to the gates of the Holy Trinity Monastery of St Sergius. Here the angel set Zachariah on the ground before the main entrance. Zachariah could see distinctly on the gates the icon of the Saviour with the open Gospel, on which was written: 'Come unto me, all ye that labour and are heavy laden, and I will give you rest' (Matt. 11.28). The Mother of God was with him, and on his right was John the Baptist. St Sergius was on the right of the icon, and Nikon* on

* Nikon (1605–1681) was a Patriarch of the Russian Orthodox Church whose reforms met with fierce opposition. Though his reforms were upheld, he himself was deposed and exiled.

the left.

Zachariah awoke and could not understand anything.

Is Moscow really like that? Is that what St Sergius's monastery and its gates really looks like? What is the meaning of Father Melchizedek's appearing to me in my dream? Oh, if only he would in real life inspire my elder Daniel to realise that my heart is not in White Shores, that I have already made a vow to labour for St Sergius.

In the morning Zachariah went into his elder's cell as he was about to drink his tea. He blessed his novice and said firmly: 'Have a good drink of tea, Zachariah, and prepare for a journey. God has given you his blessing to live in Moscow at the Holy Trinity Monastery of St Sergius.'

Obviously the will of God had been announced to the elder Daniel; perhaps the elder Melchizedek had also appeared to him during the night. Zachariah quickly began to make ready; having received the elder's blessing, he went to his home to call on his father, and from there he set off on the road to Moscow.

CHAPTER 2

The Trials of a Novice

When Zachariah arrived at the Holy Trinity Monastery of St Sergius, he was surprised to see the very same gates and the very same icons which he had seen in his dream.

Zachariah did not know a single person there, and he stayed in the monastery hostel. Here he learned from the conversation of people arriving of the existence of the elder Barnabas, who lived in the Gethsemane hermitage. Every day a mass of people thronged to him with various needs and questions. Zachariah was advised to go down to Father Barnabas to ask his advice and receive his blessing.

The young novice set off immediately. Arriving, he saw a mass of people that one could not count; they were all crowding around, wanting to see the elder, but there was no possibility of getting through to him.

But then Father Barnabas came out and said, addressing the crowd: 'If there is a monk from this monastery there, let him come here.'

No-one responded to this call, as there were no monks from the monastery in the crowd. The elder came down the staircase and said: 'Come on, let a monk from the monastery come through.' He came up to Zachariah, and took the young novice by the hand, saying affectionately: 'Well then, come into my cell.' 'I am not a monk from this monastery, I am from White Shores,' Zachariah objected. 'Yes, I know you used to live there, but now you are going to live in this monastery and be a monk here.'

Leading the overjoyed Zachariah into his cell, the elder blessed him, saying: 'Live here with St Sergius, and you will come to see me in the Gethsemane hermitage'. 'But suppose they won't accept me here?' said Zachariah. 'They'll accept

17

you. Go to the monastery gates, there are already three
superiors waiting for you there.'

After being received by the elder, Zachariah went off to the
gates, and the abbot and two other of the monastery superiors
were actually standing there. Zachariah asked them to accept
him to come and live with them in the monastery. They
accepted him willingly and Zachariah became a monk at the
monastery.

Thus was it pleasing to the Providence of the Lord to decide
Zachariah's lot.

'One must know how to distinguish dreams,' said the archi-
mandrite-*skhimnik* himself to Zachariah. 'Dreams which are
from God give the soul calmness and joy, arouse the heart to
repentance, destroy thoughts of conceit and vanity, arouse a
man to a fervent struggle with sin.' This truth is confirmed by
the facts. Zachariah's dream of the monastery and of his entering it is an example of it. It is true that it was confirmed by the
words of the elder Daniel and his blessing to set off immediately
to St Sergius's monastery, but the elder Daniel did not know
about his cell-servant's dream. The will of God for Zachariah
had been revealed to him at the same time as to Zachariah. And
now in the monastery itself the Lord had again confirmed his
will in the words of the elder Barnabas, who had called Zachariah a monk of the monastery and given him his blessing to stay
in the monastery at all costs. When the doubt crept into
Zachariah's mind that he might not be accepted, Father Barnabas said, using his powers of intuition: 'Go to the gates, there
are already three superiors waiting for you there.' The reality of
his words, the presence of the three superiors standing at the
gates and their willing acceptance of Zachariah into the number of the brothers of the Holy Trinity Monastery of St Sergius,
displayed completely and as clear as day God's Providence for
Zachariah's place of residence.

A hard life began for Zachariah from the day of his entry into
the monastery, as if he had gone there to a cross of crucifixion.
Not from one of the brothers did he see any sympathy towards
himself, and he did not make friends with anyone. Zachariah
liked to pray with a rosary, but his rosary was taken away from

him. 'You have not taken your vows yet,' they told him, 'but you pray like a monk.' Zachariah's soul was straining for prayer, he pined for it. He began to hide his rosary in his pocket, so that it would not be taken away.

Soon Zachariah started to work his way through various duties. First he went to the bakery, where he baked nearly four thousand pounds of bread a day. He was so tired that even handling things was difficult, and he was wet through from exhaustion. He changed his shirt twice a day. He slept only two hours out of twenty-four. He slept fully dressed on a wooden bench in the bakery.

Before becoming a monk, Zachariah worked his way through twenty kinds of duties. Where did he not work, what did he not endure? He was in the refectory, he was a sexton, a candlemaker, he served in cells and in the refectory, he performed every kind of monastic duty and was tormented everywhere.

However, when Zachariah became an elder and recalled the time of his novitiate, he always said: 'Glory and thanks to the Lord for everything, for everything.'

Very soon after Zachariah had settled in the monastery, a new novice from Kiev entered it, and he was also given duties in the bakery. This novice turned out to be a chronic drunkard and an inveterate criminal.

Once he got drunk to the very limit and walked through the yard staggering, carrying on outrageously, swearing in the most foul language. Zachariah's brothers said: 'Look, your novice from the bakery is coming, quite drunk. Take him to his cell.' The meek Zachariah immediately went to fulfil this order, however hard it might be for him. With difficulty he dragged the monk, who had lost all semblance of humanity, into his cell and laid him on the bed behind the screen.

Having fulfilled the order and gone into his cell, Zachariah began to listen to his heart, for from childhood he had heeded it, yielding his will and reason exclusively to the voice of the Lord, who speaks through the conscience. His heart said to the novice: 'You have drawn the latch. Unlock the door.' He did so. A short while later there suddenly came a terrible banging on the door: 'Open up, or I'll break down the door.' Zachariah said nothing. The banging grew louder and louder. Finally the door split into two and Theodore burst into Zachariah's cell, in a terrible rage. He had long hated the young monk because he did not live as he pleased. He himself could not stand the monastic life (as it turned out later, Theodore was an escaped prisoner). While living in Kiev in the guise of a monk he had killed a priest-monk and run away to Moscow; he was as it were wearing a mask, he knew how to hide himself, to lie and sham. The monastery accepted him without having the least idea of his past. When Theodore broke down the door and saw Zachariah, he fell on him like a wild beast, seized him by the throat and began to pound him against the floor, beat him and trample him with his feet. Zachariah's bones were simply cracking, his ribs were breaking, his stomach was completely crushed, and something in it snapped. Seeing that he was still alive, Theodore addressed a question to him: 'What does life or death matter to you? Cross yourself as a sign that you will not tell the superiors, kiss the icon and swear,' the murderer pronounced in a brutal voice.

Suddenly Zachariah felt within himself a fervour for the truth. 'No I won't, I won't give a false oath. You repent yourself and kiss the icon; I have already kissed the icons in the church.' 'Ah, so that's how it is,' cried the criminal, and he sat down on top of Zachariah and laid into beating and trampling him with redoubled force. Blood gushed from Zachariah's throat, nose and ears. He was covered with injuries. Theodore beat Zachariah almost lifeless, hitting him about his lower jaw, and with such force that he put his lower jaw out.

But the Lord did not abandon his chosen one. Zachariah suddenly felt within himself an unearthly strength, set his jaw back in place with his fist, seized Theodore, thrust him aside, and started running, running with all his might, out into the yard, quite beside himself, running on and on, until finally he succumbed to total weakness, lost consciousness and fell down, bathed in blood.

This happened at Christmas time. Next morning Zachariah was found and taken for dead, but when signs of life were observed he was carried off into the infirmary. For fifteen days the sufferer lay unconscious.

Subsequently the ill-starred Theodore killed another monk and was taken away from the monastery to prison in a cart.

After this assault the twenty-three-year-old Zachariah lost almost all his teeth. Already weak in health, he now became quite feeble and could not recover at all. He was assigned to lighter duties in the hospital.

There were twelve men lying there in the hospital. Zachariah felt very ill and first of all wanted to take treatment. All the patients had medicine and Zachariah began to drink them all indiscriminately, a spoonful of each medicine from each patient. How did he escape being poisoned? It is astonishing. All the time Zachariah felt a severe pain in his chest and his head. His whole body had swollen up. Zachariah looked after the patients with great love, praying ceaselessly the whole time.

There was a novice from a hermitage in the hospital. When he grew very ill, the sick man was placed on a chair, and committed his spirit to God. Before the deceased man was carried out to the mortuary, he was laid on a bed. But Zachariah, struck by the novice's quick death, began to pray to the Lord: 'O Lord, resurrect this man. All things are possible with you.' And suddenly the novice came to life, stirred and said: 'What time is it?' 'But what time do you want?' 'I need every hour . . .'

Zachariah stood there startled and moved, and in his head sounded the words: 'Believe, that whatsoever ye shall ask in my name, that will I do, that the Father may be glorified in the Son' (John 14.13). People ran to inform the doctor that the novice from the hermitage had risen from the dead, but when everyone gathered round the bed, he passed away once more.

In the same ward there was a small boy, very restless and suffering cruelly. Once Zachariah said: 'Let us read the Psalms to him.' They began to read, and the boy brightened up completely and burst out laughing, crossed himself and passed away. Some of those who were ill-disposed to Zachariah learnt what he was doing in the hospital and transferred him to other duties, first to the bakery again, then once more to the refectory. Zachariah's health did not improve; he had been severely maimed by Theodore.

Zachariah wanted very much to die, once he had taken the form of an angel, that is, his monk's vows. He went to Father Barnabas and said: 'The novice beat me, I shall die, I shall not live to take the monastic vows. Admit me to my monastic cloak in secret.' 'No, it should not be done secretly,' said the elder, 'you shall be a monk openly. I forbid you to receive treatment from doctors or to take medicines. Live like this: bear your illness with gratitude, ask help only from the Lord. I shall vouch for you before God, and you will live to be a hundred years old. If you turn to the doctors, you will not live that long, you will die earlier. But you will not die soon, you will receive everything in your time; you will be a deacon and a priest-monk and the confessor of all the brothers of the monastery.'

Zachariah began his duties in the refectory. Here he had a great deal of work. He tried to carry out his duties thoroughly, as if before the face of the Lord.

Once a little old man, thin but fine-looking, came into the refectory. At that moment Zachariah was carrying a breast of calf and a head of cabbage. Seeing the old man, he stopped, asked for his blessing and gave him something to eat. Acts of charity came especially naturally to Zachariah's young soul, as his mother had accustomed him to them from childhood. The old man said to Zachariah: 'You have a good duty here, but prepare yourself, for soon you will be required to go to St Sergius.' And in fact in 1875 Zachariah did receive the new duty of standing at St Sergius's shrine. He carried out this task for three and a half years.

Zachariah wanted to work his way through other duties too and he turned to St Sergius: 'Give me your blessing to labour at other duties too.' So he begged the Saint, and soon after he was moved to be a candle-seller at the site of three sets of relics, those of St Serapion, St Ioasaf and St Dionysius. Here he had to sell candles, polish the floors, clean the shrines of the saints with sand, and as well as all these duties to stand constantly at the candle-counter.

In 1879 our toiler was transferred to the refectory as a sexton. Almost ten years had passed since Zachariah had moved into the monastery. Many of his contemporaries had taken monastic vows long ago. Zachariah's heart burned with love towards the Lord, he wanted very much to take the tonsure too, so that in the ranks of the angels he could yield himself to God even more fervently. But many of the monks did not like him. The time when he was living in the monastery was a time of decline in the monks' spiritual zeal. Some of them were monks only in outward appearance, and lived an entirely worldly life; they took wives for themselves, ate meat, saved up money, did not give alms, prayed only for show and then only with their lips, and had no enthusiasm at all for the honour of acquiring the monastic virtues. They did little labour, and some became complete parasites. As for the goal of Christian feats and the Christian life in general, and the possession of the Holy Spirit in their hearts, they completely forgot about them.

They spoke of Zachariah like this: 'If you lived like normal people, Zachariah, you would have been a monk long ago, but you play at being holier-than-thou, you pray all the time, never go out anywhere, invite people in to you, feed them and give advice . . . and that's not all . . . look what kind of a man you've turned out to be . . .'

Zachariah steadfastly remembered the words of his elder, Father Barnabas: 'You will be a deacon and a priest-monk and the confessor of all the brothers of the monastery.'

His heart was always inclined only towards the Lord, and he laid all his hope upon him: 'Put not your trust in princes, nor in the son of man, in whom there is no help.'*

Cursed is the man who puts his hope in man, and blessed is he who hopes in the Lord. Blessed is the man who has spurned all worldly hope and laid all his hope on the Lord. A heart attuned like this can raise up fervent prayers to the Lord and to his Most Pure Mother.

One time the young spiritual leader was standing in the church, where the miracle-working icon of St Nicholas was kept, the very same icon which had been damaged by a shot in 1608. All I know is that in that year in Russia the monastery came under fire. A shot pierced the iron door and struck St

* Psalm 145.3, (Psalm 146.3 in the English Bible, which numbers the Psalms differently from the Russian Bible. Translator's note).

Nicholas's cheek, and a splinter rebounding from it hit the Archangel Michael's crown. They searched for it later, but simply could not find it. No-one knows where it vanished.

Once Zachariah stood in this church by the icon of the Saviour, weeping and earnestly praying that the Lord would grant him the favour of receiving the rank of a monk.

At that moment two pilgrims came into the church. One was very old, the other young, probably in his early thirties. They had just stood through the mass. The young one, catching sight of Zachariah, stopped and said: 'Why are you grieving over monkhood? There are people higher than monks in the world. Do not grieve. And moreover, you have the hope of achieving monkhood.'

Zachariah invited the pilgrims in to drink tea. They accepted and came. Zachariah set out refreshments for them but they touched almost nothing. Zachariah asked the pilgrims to stay in the monastery until he took the tonsure.

'Stay for a while, and then you will know what my name as a monk will be.' The young pilgrim said: 'Your name has been written down long ago and is lying in a book.'

And in fact Zachariah thought all the time about monkhood and a long time before this had written down the name which he wanted to bear as a monk, 'Zosima'. He had placed this name in the Gospel, secretly hoping that the Lord would hear his wish and fulfil his request. The young pilgrim, who had scarcely entered Zachariah's cell and had not touched any of his things, already knew everything, even this secret action of his.

When the pilgrims had gone, Zachariah had an unusual feeling. 'I don't know what has happened to me,' he thought, recalling how as he sat between the two pilgrims he had burned as if in a fire. 'It is impossible to convey what I have experienced,' he thought, 'only the Holy Spirit coming down from heaven can give a man such a sensation. Surely it could not have been the Holy Trinity that came to me?' he pondered. 'The Father, the Son and the Holy Spirit. I never felt anything like it before in my heart, never such burning, such power, which my heart perceived when the Father and the Son were with me and when my heart sensed the Holy Spirit!

'But what am I thinking, perhaps this is not true. Perhaps it is my imagination? How dare I think like this? Maybe these were ordinary pilgrims, and only appeared to me to be something else?'

So thought the meek, modest youth, treating visions very carefully, for he steadfastly remembered that the enemy often tempts men even by this means.

One may fall into error with the least fit of imagination or self-importance, take a vision of the enemy to be a true one and succumb to captivity by the enemy and to conceit.

'Oh, if only they would come to me again,' he thought, 'if I could find out who they are, angels or men? I will ask the Lord to reveal to me who they are. If they are angels, then let the young pilgrim, when he arrives here, read something from the Epistles, the Gospels and the Psalter, quite spontaneously, without any request from me, or let him make me read, and that will be a sign that they are not ordinary pilgrims but angels, sent to make us sinners understand and repent.'

The pilgrims had been with Zachariah on 27 February. Zachariah also remembered that the young pilgrim's face had undergone a surprising change. In the church it had been fine-looking, not drawn at all, but rather plump, but as soon as he entered the cell his face became thin, even emaciated.

The second half of March arrived. Once again Zachariah saw the same two pilgrims. They stood through the mass and when it ended they set off to see the deacon, but he had guests just then and was relaxing, so it was inconvenient for him to receive visitors. The deacon knew that Zachariah loved all the poor, the beggars, the grief-stricken and the pilgrims, so he thought of sending them to him. 'Go to Father Zachariah, he will give you a drink of tea.'

As soon as the pilgrims entered Father Zachariah's cell, the younger one pulled a small book from out of his clothing, opened it and ordered Zachariah to read the Epistle to the Romans chapter one, verses 1 to 25 inclusive, ending with the words: 'who is blessed for ever. Amen.'

After the reading from the Epistle, the pilgrim made

Zachariah read the Gospel, from John chapter 14, pericope 47, verses 1 to 31 inclusive.

Zachariah read the whole of this chapter, finishing with the words: 'Arise, let us go hence.'

While Zachariah was reading this chapter, the young pilgrim's tears were pouring down.

After the reading of the Gospel, the pilgrim asked: 'What is that large book you have lying there?' 'That is the Psalter.' 'Then read Psalm 90.'* Zachariah read this amazing psalm and then read several more psalms.

'Oh, if only someone understood properly the meaning of the Psalter.'

'Then read the commentary to the Psalter.'

Zachariah followed all that was happening with emotion, and he felt with all his soul that his prayerful entreaties had been fulfilled, that the Lord Himself was confirming that these pilgrims were from God, that this was no flight of imagination, no bewitching, but a vision. It was a miracle from God. While he was reading the Psalter, Zachariah prayed to the Mother of God: 'Diligent Protectress, Mother of the Most High God' (the anthem of Our Lady of Kazan). With his whole heart Zachariah offered up this amazing prayer to the Mother of God, praying by himself in his thoughts.

This inward activity was not concealed from the pilgrim: 'Here is prayer being offered to the Mother of God . . . we were in grief and he called . . . he heard us and pardoned us.'

The pilgrim said: 'Brother, remember me in your prayers in two years time and bow three times . . . remember me in ten years time and bow three times . . . and again in twenty years time and bow three times . . .'

'I won't live twenty years,' replied Zachariah, 'I am ill.'

The pilgrim made no reply to these words and began to say: 'Bishop, prelate, you won't understand yet but you will later . . . Here is what will happen within two years, brother – cities, provinces, Peter, and then very quickly you will come back. You will have three crosses, three crosses.'

Soon after this Zachariah was admitted to the lowest monas-

* Psalm 89 in the English translation of the Bible. (Translator's note.)

tic rank, with the name of Zosima.

Two years later Father Zosima was sent to Petersburg by Metropolitan Ioannikios, who took him on as his assistant. Here in the church he saw the icon of the Holy Trinity, of enormous dimensions. He felt in his spirit the grace which had illumined him during the pilgrims' visit. Greatly moved, he made three bows and fell down onto his knees before the icon of the Holy Trinity.

In fact Father Zosima stayed a very short time in Petersburg; he was very soon sent back, thanks to his illiteracy. So the pilgrim's words were fulfilled: 'In two years time bow three times, in two years time, cities, provinces, Peter and then you will return. . .'

Ten years later Father Zosima was ordained deacon and was sent again to Petersburg, where he saw the same icon of the Holy Trinity once more, and bowed three times before it. And twenty years later, in the church of the Most Holy Trinity in the Danilov Monastery in Moscow, Father Zosima was ordained archimandrite. Bishop Seraphim Chichagov ordained him. Thus all the times appointed by the pilgrim were fulfilled.

Father Zosima actually did receive the three crosses of which the pilgrim spoke. The first was the Tsar's cross, the second the Synod's cross and the third an archimandrite's cross.

After the reading from the Epistle, the Gospel and the Psalter, and having foretold for Zachariah the times of the most important events of his life, the pilgrims prepared to leave. The young pilgrim took an icon (given with the blessing of the elder Barnabas) and blessed Zachariah with it.

After this they vanished.

The third time the young pilgrim appeared to Father Zachariah alone. At that moment Father Zachariah was in his cell, together with another monk. The young pilgrim entered through the closed door, blessed and kissed them. Father Zachariah asked him to taste some food with them, but when he looked at him he was horrified – the young pilgrim had become as transparent as the bright sunlight and was shining with an inexpressible beauty, impossible to communicate in words.

Father Zachariah and his friend, the other monk, saw that he was standing on clouds. They began to tremble and fell face forwards onto their knees, but he disappeared from their sight. 'O miracle! O the divine majesty and boundlessness of his mercy. Yes, wonderful are thy ways, O Lord.'

Zachariah experienced painful moments, when his heart was torn with pain, when thoughts burst into his head like black crows and devoured his inner self. But our spiritual leader, armed with prayer, struggled courageously with them like a bold warrior and did not submit to their yoke. Zachariah's difficulties increased because he had to worry not only about those lesser than him, but also about those who were higher than him.

For several years he had been the cell-servant of the elder Nicholas (called Nicanor as a *skhimnik*). Zachariah concerned himself not only with the outward orderliness of the cell and all the affairs of his elder, but, most of all, with the salvation of the soul of his superior, who had the misfortune to be a hoarder of money. With touching love he begged Father Nicholas to give away all his possessions to the poor, to submit and give away his thousands and all his things that had any value. Father Nicholas submitted in spirit and confessed all his sins and thoughts to his cell-servant Father Zachariah, even though at that time Father Zachariah was only a novice. 'I am not your elder, you will be my elder,' he often said.

Father Nicholas passed away to God in peace, having broken all earthly ties at the insistence of his young elder-cum-cell-servant Father Zachariah. The more Zachariah excelled in virtue, the more the enemy of the human race took up arms against him, attacking him through people who hated spiritual zeal.

Those of the monks who by their sins were trampling their rank underfoot could not bear to see Father Zachariah and mocked him unspeakably, and many of them even played unthinkable tricks on him. Some of them, seeing his total estrangement from the world and his living faith, which is oneness with the unseen world, were afraid of him and, hating the righteous man, wished to banish him somewhere farther away.

'Oh you God's fool, you're as thick as two planks, unspeakable, you don't live like everyone else but act holier-than-thou' – these and similar epithets were showered on the young but staunch zealot, who was striving towards the only thing which is the purpose of the Christian life – the possession of the Holy Spirit.

Here we are describing a time of extreme decline in monasticism, when some monks did not keep their vows, did not answer to their rank, and could not even be called monks.

But side by side with this dismal spectacle some of the monks nonetheless flourished and were fragrant with the purity of childhood and of all the Christian virtues, but it was hard for them, very hard. One of these martyrs was Father Zachariah, whom we are describing here.

Before he was ordained priest he was given another duty, that of cell-servant to Father Nicholas, a priest-monk and *skhimnik*. Father Nicholas was pensive and dull. He had many possessions in his cell, and he did not fulfil the monastic vows. He liked to hoard money, and all sorts of unnecessary possessions, and also things which pleased him alone, crammed his living quarters, just as superfluous things cram the flats of worldly people.

Then Father Nicholas fell ill, fatally ill. Oh God, what a terrible illness it was. He suffered as though he were in hell, and not so much from physical pains as from mental and moral ones. His conscience tormented him so much that he cried out at the top of his voice from pain of soul: 'Father Zosima, Father Zosima, put me to death, I cannot be tormented any more . . .' 'Elder, what are you saying, life is eternal, and death is an amplification and intensification of the life of the soul. You will make your torments all the harder if you do not acknowledge your sins. Repent before it is too late; I see you have a mass of unnecessary possessions, give them away to the poor. It is indispensable for you to distribute your things first, ungrudgingly, for all the same you have no longer to live on the earth. Repent, give alms, for there is no mercy for him who gives no mercy . . . Blessed are the merciful, for they shall receive mercy.'

Father Zosima handed the dying man the Gospel to kiss,

saying: 'It will make you feel better.' But he threw the Gospel onto the floor.

'What is wrong with you? You have thrown to the floor the book through which the Saviour always speaks to us, around which angels are always flying.'

In a kind of desperation the monk sobbed as if in a frenzy, tore his clothing and groaned: 'Oh, oh, you don't know what a sinner I am, let me unburden my soul to you. I will bring you my repentance and you will plead with God for me, not to torment me as I am now being tormented. Oh, what are these torments here compared with the everlasting, never-ending torments of hell.'

'Elder, I will call your confessor and you can repent.'

'Be silent, I do not want a confessor. I will not reveal my soul to anyone, except to you. Accept my repentance, otherwise I shall kill myself. I don't know what I shall do, I am burning all over in fire from the torments of Gehenna. I have shrunk, I have shrunk, Father Zosima, although you are still young and I am an old man, but when you are a confessor you will forgive my sins. Listen, I beg you.'

Father Zosima submitted, but, O God, what did he not hear from the elder. He had not revealed his sins out of shame and fear, but had come to the Holy Sacraments, to communion, and in taking communion had entered into judgement and condemnation. The unhappy man had grown twisted and contorted from the pain of the torments of his soul.

Father Zosima knelt before the icon of the Queen of Heaven and, bursting into tears, begged her to have mercy on the repenting sinner. And he promised Nicholas that if he should be asked another time on his behalf, he would forgive his sins, if he had the right to do so. He begged him to begin to do works of charity before it was too late.

Father Nicholas agreed and soon the entire cell of the dying man and all the things that were in it had passed into the hands of the poor. All the money which he had been saving all his life was also given away to those who had nothing. And the elder died peacefully, whispering a prayer of repentance . . .

Many years later the elder recounted to me with great grief

the drama of the unhappy Father Nicholas. I asked him: 'Did you forgive his sins, Father?' 'Not yet, I gave alms for him and prayed, but are you asking me to forgive him? – are you asking?' 'Yes, I am asking.' 'In that case I forgive all his sins on your account, for all his life, and I give you my blessing to pray all your life for his repose, and, as much as you are able, to do good works for him.'

One day Father Zosima was given the task of collecting money for the monastery from passers-by at railway stations.

Father Zosima took a stick and humbly set off to where he was told to go. 'Well, there's a good task for him, let him play the God's fool,' the monks laughed at him.

Despite the many years he had spent in the monastery, not a word was said about his ordination.

So there was Father Zosima sitting at the station with a bowl, when suddenly a young child not more than three months old stood before him, watching him. Father Zosima looked at him with a kind of special feeling of reverence, and finally decided to start a conversation with him, curious to know where he had appeared from. 'Tell me something. Will I be a deacon?' 'You will,' the child pronounced clearly and distinctly. 'And a priest-monk?' 'Yes.' 'And an archimandrite?' 'Yes.' 'Well, he'll probably answer "yes" to all my questions,' thought Father Zosima, 'so I'd better ask him if I shall be a Metropolitan.' 'No, you will not,' replied the child. 'Why not?' 'God has ordered it so,' he said, and vanished.

'It must have been an angel or the Saviour himself,' said the elder, crossing himself. Such were the wonderful miracles by which the Lord strengthened his suffering spiritual leader, Father Zosima.

A little while later Father Zosima was sent to Metropolitan Ioannikios. Before his departure Father Zosima went to his elder, Father Barnabas and received his blessing to go away and his advice not to unpack his belongings, since he would have to ride back on the return journey.

And in fact that is what happened. (I have written about this in the description of the miracle of the appearance of the Holy Trinity to Father Zosima.)

After his return to the monastery Zachariah and a few other monks spent three years engaged in various studies with the archimandrite, and then sat examinations, thus completing their general education.

CHAPTER 3

Victory over Adversity

Zosima's ordination seemed to be performed by the Lord himself, in spite of all possible obstacles, which were placed in his way by people who hated a righteous life.

Not long before his ordination, he received a letter from his confessor, Father Andrew Shcheglov, whose name as a *skhimnik* was Father Abraham. He wrote as follows: 'My dear friend, I thought it would not fall to your lot to enter holy orders, but it has turned out otherwise. The Queen of Heaven herself will elevate you to the first rank, to the diaconate, and when you have reached that, you will prepare for the second step, the priest-monkhood.' The time came for him to receive holy orders, and, contrary to everyone's expectations, complete outsiders began to remind the superiors of the monastery of the modest monk whom the Queen of Heaven herself had predestined for ordination.

Near the St Sergius Monastery lived a devout colonel's wife, Catherine Andreevna, who had dedicated her life to God. Everyone in the monastery knew and respected her. Inspired from above, she came to the Abbot and the other superiors one day and said: 'Why do you always pass over Father Zosima? He is_more than worthy of the priesthood, but you are ordaining boys.'

To this the head of the monastery replied: 'He took holiness upon himself, and in our monastery we don't like saints. If Father Zosima had been like everyone else, he would have been a priest-monk long ago.' 'Oh you dogs,' exclaimed Catherine Andreevna indignantly, 'what do you live in a monastery for if you don't love holiness? You have lost the image of monkhood, you take wives, you indulge in drunkenness and debauchery.'

Soon after Catherine Andreevna's denunciation of the life of the monks in the monastery, a nun arrived from Shamordin, a spiritual daughter of Father Ambrose. Her outward appearance was formidable, and in her hands she held a huge staff, like a crozier. She denounced the superiors sharply. 'Oh you monsters, you have killed Father Zosima, at least ordain him now, before he passes on to the Lord. He is extremely ill.'

These and similar reminders on the part of outsiders and those living a truly monastic life simply showered down on the monks who bitterly hated and were mercilessly persecuting the righteous man.

Father Zosima was advised to stand up for himself. 'No,' he replied, '"put not your trust in princes, nor in the son of man, in whom there is no help."* I have set my hope on the One God and on his Most Pure Mother.'

There and then he was ordained as a deacon, and in a short time as a priest-monk. He was ordained by the Right Reverend Trifon, who had known Father Zosima for a long time and respected and loved him. After receiving holy orders, the duty of being the general confessor for the monastery was laid upon him.

There were five different abbots while Father Zosima was living in the monastery. He entered it in Father Antony's time, and it was then that he had the duty of standing by the relics of St Sergius. Under the abbot Father Leonid, on 4 April, Father Zachariah was admitted to the lowest monastic order with the name of Zosima. As Father Andrew had written to him and as the elder Barnabas had foretold to him: 'Not a year will go by before you receive your monk's cloak,' and in fact Father Zosima was vested in his cloak on 9 March.

On that day ten men, including Zosima, became monks.

They spent several days in the church, taking Communion and praying, and when they came out Father Zosima suggested to the new monks that they should go down to worship at the icon of Our Lady of Chernigov and to see the elder Barnabas. Five agreed to go, but five remained at home, and moreover one of them spoke very rudely of the elder Barnabas: 'Why on earth should I go? What am I going to do with that false prophet

* Psalm 145.3 (Psalm 146.3 in the English Bible).

Barnabas?'

'Oh, woe betide you, you wretch,' said Father Zosima and began to sob. 'You are the most wretched of all of us.'

What happened to this monk, whose name was Nahum, will be told later.

And so five remained at home, like the foolish virgins, and five set off for the elder Barnabas's cell. They all wanted very much to see him, but this was very difficult, since there were crowds of people waiting, and by no means all could be received.

They stood through a service at the miracle-working icon of Our Lady of Chernigov, and afterwards they turned to Father Zosima and began to ask him: 'Pray to the Queen of Heaven that the elder Barnabas will receive us all; pray to Our Lady, for who is nearer to her than you are? We all know that your life is passed under her protection, that you make your every movement with her blessing, that her will and the will of her son, our Saviour, is everything to you.'

At first Father Zosima refused: 'What are you saying? I am a sinner; you can pray better to the Queen of Heaven.' But the entreaties were so forceful that he yielded and prayed to the Mother of God: 'Queen of Heaven, Most Pure Lady, let us through to the elder, let him receive us, bless and exhort each one separately. Let each one find out about himself that which he needs to know. Queen of Heaven, hear us.'

After this prayer, everyone turned their steps towards Father Barnabas's hut. The elder came out into the doorway as if he were waiting for the monks, and despite the huge crowd, said affectionately to them: 'Welcome, holy fathers. Father Gregory, put on the samovar and give these great elders a drink.' Everyone except Father Zosima sat down at the table. He, however, standing to one side by a chest of drawers, examined the crosses and icons which the elder gave away to visitors.

Father Barnabas addressed him with the words: 'But you, Zosima, wherever you may sit, will all the same be the confessor of the whole brotherhood, despite the fact that you became a monk later than them. On the other hand, you will survive everyone and the time will come when you will remain alone in the monastery.'

And in fact Father Zosima called as a *skhimnik* Father Zachariah, lived to a ripe old age and survived almost all his contemporaries, and he lived longer than everyone in the Holy Trinity Monastery. When all the monks were driven out, Zosima did not leave the monastery, and was the very last to go from it.

'And three of you, fathers, will wear gold crosses,* and two will be proto-deacons.'

Everything turned out according to the elder's words.

A little while later two of the new monks did in fact die in the rank of proto-deacon, and three rose to obtain their gold crosses.

Yes, Barnabas was a great elder. Father Zosima went to him for thirty years for advice on various matters, and afterwards he would often say: 'I myself achieved nothing, but I saw many people who did achieve something.'

But what happened to the monk who had spoken so rudely of the elder Barnabas?

This is what befell him. For disobedience to his superiors he was banished to the Nikolaev hermitage. He completely failed to understand the way of monasticism, that it is a continual bearing of the cross, crucifixion of oneself, renunciation of one's will. It is martyrdom. He did not consider disobedience to be a great sin against monasticism, but thought that he was being unjustly ill-treated. The enemy was swift to seize his soul, which was unprepared for a struggle, and drove him to despair.

Left in a gloomy, half-ruined cell in the Nikolaev hermitage, he went completely out of his mind, seized a knife that was lying on the floor after potato-peeling and cut his throat. As he lay there dying in terrible torment, he wheezed and blamed others for his death.

When Father Zosima learnt of this, his loving heart contracted painfully. He took this dreadful death very hard indeed.

Father Zosima declared to the superiors of the monastery: 'You are guilty of the despair and death of Nahum, so at least

* The gold cross signifies an elevation in status from the basic grade of priest. (Translator's note.)

pray now for his soul.'

After long and earnest prayers for him, Father Zosima saw in a dream the wretched man who had perished. He was walking along with his face turned away, wearing dirty clothing, torn to ribbons. Around him were leaping demons with staves and lances. 'Where is your monk's cloak?' Father Zosima asked him. 'I haven't got it,' replied Nahum. 'Give me yours.' Father Zosima took off his monk's robe and covered the half-naked suicide with it.

Father Zosima carried out his task as the general confessor for the monastery. He had a reverential attitude towards the great sacrament of confession, established as early as the moment in the Garden of Eden when the Lord spoke to Adam and Eve, after their fall, summoning them to confess their sin to him.

Father Zosima always acknowledged all the Saviour's great mercy and ineffable love to us, shown in the establishment of the sacrament of confession.

He was never in a hurry to let anyone go from confession, and there were occasions when he gave three and a half hours of his time to one person. There were sinners who revealed their entire lives and begged for guidance and advice in all their different kinds of needs and circumstances. However, the majority of confessors at that time were more concerned with chasing after money than with the salvation of human souls. 'Oh, Father Zosima, you don't know how to hear confession,' they jeered at him. 'You spent the whole service with one person, but I collected a whole thirty-eight roubles in that time.'

The monks utterly flouted the vow of poverty. One such case occurred with Antony, a superior of the monastery. A pilgrim arrived, an old woman from Smolensk province, poor and exhausted. She went up to the shrine of St Sergius and asked for a service to be said to him. 'Give me thirty kopeks,' said the monk. 'I haven't got it, dear father, so please say the service for this piece of gingham.' 'What would I want with your gingham? Go and sell it, and then come back tomorrow and I'll say the service.' The old woman was not offended and did not blame anyone, but went sadly out of the church. 'I have given a vow to say the service, but evidently I am unworthy. Just who am I going to sell this gingham to?' Suddenly she saw an old man with a kind of radiance in his face coming along. 'What are you selling, my dear? Give it to me, here are thirty kopeks for you.' The old woman was overjoyed, and went into the alms-house, where they gave her shelter, and waited on tenterhooks for the following day.

Next morning the monks who were on duty came into the church and tried to open the shrine with the relics, but it would not yield, it seemed to have been locked with some kind of secret key. They sent for the abbot, who prayed fervently, and at last the shrine opened. To their surprise, they saw in the shrine the piece of gingham, which the Saint seemed to be holding in his hand.

'What is this? Where did it come from? Who took the service yesterday?' The monk who had refused the old woman the pre-vious day said: 'I have sinned, this is what happened to me yes-terday,' and related everything to do with the old woman. They sent for her. 'Is this your piece of gingham?' 'It is mine. An old man bought it from me, but how it got into the shrine I don't know.'

'Yes, this is the man who bought it,' said the old woman, pointing to a large icon of St Sergius. The charity of St Sergius towards the old woman, and the unmasking of the greedy monk, became clear to them all.

Father Zosima entreated people not to love possessions and on no account to hoard money. There was a monk in the mon-astery called Father Theoktist who had hoarded several thou-sand roubles. Father Zosima found out about this and began to entreat him: 'Disperse the goods you have collected here. Give away your money to the poor, make donations to the church, and so on.' Father Theoktist obeyed, and after his death only twenty roubles remained in his cell.

Father Theoktist appeared in a dream to Father Zosima from the other world and asked him to give away the remaining twenty roubles to the poor for the remembrance of his soul. The elder Zosima did not know about these twenty roubles, since others were living in Father Theoktist's cell and the money had been hidden.

There was another monk like him in the monastery, who had hoarded seven thousand roubles. Not only did he not help anyone, he would not even lend anyone a single kopek. Father Zosima knew that it means death for the soul of a monk who has taken the vow of poverty if he flouts that vow and gives himself up to the passion of greed for money. His heart bled for his brother who had fallen into sin and he began lovingly to persuade him to repent, saying: 'You will die in a few months, you know, so give alms.' Father Silvester, as the monk was called, did not agree. 'Repent, my dear friend,' Father Zosima tried to persuade him. 'Give alms and then you will go to paradise. I beg you, with pity and love for your soul, to do this. Repent, for soon you will go out of your mind and die.' But it was all in vain. Soon Father Silvester did in fact go mad, and died in the summer. His faith was very weak. Once, not long before Silvester's death, the elder offered to read him an acathist.* 'What on earth are you saying? Am I some old woman from the backwoods who wants to read an acathist?' 'Oh, you are inclined to blasphemy,' said Father Zosima sorrowfully, 'surely you know that acathists confront men's souls with the grandeur of holiness and spiritual heroism and bring them delight and tenderness?'

After his death Father Silvester appeared to Father Zosima in a dream and tried to stifle him, showing that he was being stifled and tormented by his unrepented sins, and that it was wretchedly hard for him in the other world.

Father Zosima increased his prayers and alms for him.

One day the abbot sent Father Zosima to see Father Agafon. It was a long way to the hermitage and Father Zosima went by the shortest route, across the pond. The water had already disappeared, and there was snow and ice on the banks. Father Zosima crossed himself and set off, taking a very long staff in his hand. On the banks there was no trouble and he walked along, but when he went just a little further the staff plunged downwards and Father Zosima found himself in the water. It was

* An acathist is a church service held in honour of the Mother of God. Sometimes acathists are also served to Christ. (Translator's note.)

over twenty feet deep. Father Zosima pulled out his staff and boldly began to walk on the water. He did it as a work of penance, reciting a prayer and pressing to his breast the sacred objects he had with him. From the monastic community on the bank a deacon of the hermitage was watching him with great surprise. Who was this walking on the water across the pond? Recognising Father Zosima, the deacon shouted: 'Father Zosima, what is this, have you started to perform miracles?'

'Forgive me, father, I thought the water was frozen and first of all I walked over frozen water, but then further on the ice had melted. But I walked across as an act of penance, and I had with me the icons of St Zosima and St Savvati and the Host of the Mother of God, and because of this the Lord held me up.'

'Who can possibly believe it?' Father Zosima would say, recounting the second occasion when he walked on the water. 'But as I am a priest, I speak the truth, I was dry when I walked out onto the bank, and not even my boots were wet'.

But these miracles, obvious mercies from God, revealed to Father Zosima the pure in heart, had no effect on his enemies, who were blinded by their passions.

After Abbot Paul, a good, responsive man, Father Tobias was installed.

Father Tobias's time in office is a distressing memory. Under him the entire spiritual life of the monastery went into a great decline. Abbot Tobias bore an improbable hatred for Father Zosima and systematically mocked him. Twice he made an attempt on Father Zosima's life through other people. Even in little things Father Tobias injured Father Zosima. When Father Zosima began to direct queues of people, he took away his collecting box. Father Zosima served without pay for fifteen years, for Father Tobias allotted him not a single kopek.

But Father Zosima thanked God for everything, prayed for his enemies and did not condemn them, realising that it was the devil himself that was attacking him through men. He had pity on those who offended him and hated primordial evil more and more. The enemy especially hates charity, but the cruel Abbot Tobias ordered the poor to be thrown out on their ears.

Father Zosima had the greatest love for the least of his fellowmen, seeing the Lord himself in them. 'Surely we should not throw out the poor, it is just the same as throwing out Christ himself', Father Zosima would say.

Incited by Father Tobias, his friend Anfim suggested one day that Father Zosima should buy a wardrobe from him, but the latter refused. Then Anfim asked Father Zosima to help him move the wardrobe. With unusual strength, Anfim pushed the wardrobe towards Father Zosima and it fell on him at full force. Father Zosima found himself lying on the floor underneath the wardrobe. Then, put up to it by Father Tobias, the monk purposely began to strike Father Zosima. 'What are you doing, you know you'll kill me,' shouted Father Zosima. At this Anfim burst out laughing with a kind of devilish laughter. It was a good thing that at this moment a visitor who had arrived came in and helped Father Zosima to free himself from the wardrobe that was crushing him.

Father Zosima prayed diligently for this brother of his, who soon went out of his mind and died. A little while later in a dream he saw Anfim, who came up to him and began to kiss his hand.

The forgiving Father Zosima prayed also for Father Tobias, that the Lord would humble him, and that he would change his way of thinking if only a little, so that his soul would not perish.

Several more attempts were made on Father Zosima's life. One day a staircase was pulled out from underneath him and Father Zosima was seriously hurt. In the bath-house boiling water was poured over him. Father Zosima was mocked in every way, and beaten up by anyone who chose to with whatever he chose. When Father Zosima asked: 'Why on earth are you beating me?', the reply was: 'To make you stop living as you do and live like everyone else. Stop imitating the saints. If you try to climb up among the saints, then we'll beat you; the saints were always beaten.' They even went as far as calling Father Zosima a madman and made an attempt to drag him off to a lunatic asylum.

'So what, the Lord is in the lunatic asylum too. Do with me what you will, but I will not live in your way. I have a duty to obey the dictates of my conscience and live according to the commandments of God.'

It was intolerably hard for Father Zosima to bear all these wrongful attacks through the medium of embittered enemies, his very own monks. He went to his elder, Father Barnabas, to ask him to give him his blessing to move to another monastery.

'No,' replied the elder Barnabas, 'you cannot have my blessing for this. Live here, don't go away anywhere and save yourself. Only don't hoard money, don't drink wine and don't take medicine.' So the long-suffering Father Zosima remained in the monastery.

Father Zosima's prayer about the unworthy Father Tobias was heard. It happened, in a way that was very useful for Father Tobias, that he took flight from the place in twenty-four hours. The local authorities sent him into retirement. Father Tobias's embarrassment and chagrin knew no limit. He tried to conceal his merited disgrace and, under the guise of illness, resigned as Abbot. The monastery hated him so much that he could not live near it, and went further away.

Having spent some time in retirement, Father Tobias began to grow submissive. Twice he visited Father Zosima and begged in tears for forgiveness. Once he went to the church where Father Zosima was taking a service and asked the sexton: 'Who is going to take the Mass?' 'Father Zosima,' he was told. 'Then tell him to wait for me tomorrow, in case I am late; I want to take Communion at his service.' In his time as abbot he would not even receive him into the same service as himself. But now at the altar he begged forgiveness again and again. Soon he became a *skhimnik*, and died.

After Father Tobias's death, Father Kronits was abbot. He also had an indifferent attitude to Father Zosima, but, realising his qualities as an elder, he made him confessor of the entire brotherhood of the monastery. Under him Father Zosima received his cross and his *nabedrennik*.*

Father Zosima's loving heart had to endure much, far too much, that was painful when he looked at the degradation of his brothers, and he hated the enemy of the human race more and

* A *nabedrennik* is a rectangle borne by high-ranking priests on their side. (Translator's note.)

more. His love for weak, ill, unhappy, lost, tormented people grew and grew. He welcomed them into his cell like a mother, consoled, fed, encouraged and taught them. He was persecuted for this, and forbidden to receive people, but he fulfilled the Saviour's commandment: 'Love one another' and did not deviate from his path, despite all the stones that were thrown at him.

The most Pure Mother of God herself appeared to him in a dream and gave him her blessing to receive the people. He yielded himself entirely to the Lord, walking along the straight and narrow way.

'Sometimes a man does not know himself what he will say,' the elder used to remark. 'The Lord himself speaks through his lips. One must pray like this: "O Lord, may you live in me, may you speak through me, may you act through me." When the Lord speaks through a man's lips, then all the words of that man are effective and all that is spoken by him is fulfilled. The man who is speaking is himself surprised at this. It is necessary only to have firm faith and to yield one's heart and lips to the Lord. "I shall not speak a word of my own outside your will, do with me what you will" – this is how to pray. Only then one must not rely on wisdom, one must have the kind of wisdom that gives the Lord access, so that he can do what he wants with one.

'Do not strive after wealth, do not seek anything on this earth. Give your soul to hell and you will be rich.

'Live honestly, and remember that we do not have a permanent city here, but are seeking the one to come.'

One day Father Zosima was reading the Life of Theodora, the spiritual daughter of Basil the New, and the afflictions she passed through. This is a moving tale, which every Christian must bear in his heart. At this moment he was invited to drink tea, and the deacon Ambrose and the novice Michael sat down at the table. Michael took up the book and continued reading. Father Ambrose, smiling sceptically, said: 'Are you a believer?' Father Zosima looked at him in deep sorrow and said: 'Why then did you once become a monk?'

'O Christians,' Father Zosima would often say, 'we live in

such a worldly way and take no thought for eternity, but we really must take thought. Walk before the face of the Lord, and remember that your every good action is recorded by your Guardian Angel, appointed by the Lord to look after you, but every sin is recorded by the dark power. You should not do anything hidden, so that it will not become manifest. Repent before it is too late, humble yourself and save your soul. Read the Gospels, read them as you should, try to steep yourself in them. You must knead these words well, in order that they may enter your heart. Strive to be Christ's disciples, that the Spirit of God may be in you: "Learn of me; for I am meek and lowly in heart: and ye shall find rest unto your souls" (Matt. 11.29). You must love people in deed and in truth, not by word and by the tongue. You must learn to love people as yourself, that is, to show to others the same all-forgiving love and care that you show to yourself. Watch that you do not give alms for show, and do not glorify yourself, like a Pharisee. But do give alms every day. The day when you do not give alms is lost for eternity, it is lost for your soul. Alms help us to receive the grace of the Holy Spirit. "Blessed are the merciful: for they shall obtain mercy." (Matt. 5.7). Alms can extricate the soul of a sinner even from hell. The angel of this virtue stands perpetually before the throne of the Lord and sings of the alms that have been given. "Take therefore no thought for the morrow; for the morrow shall take thought for the things of itself. Sufficient unto the day is the evil thereof" (Matt. 6.34).

'Look on every day you live as the last day of your life. Always remember that the Lord watches you and sees your every action, every thought and feeling. Hate sins, for they are the greatest evil of all. Sin gave birth to the devil. Sin causes us to fall into the Gehenna of fiery torments, tearing us away from the Lord God in the One Trinity.

'Our hearts, once they have fallen into hell, are worse than they would be in the torments of every kind of suffering, and they will grieve for ever over the grace that has been lost. So be good and careful, little children, do not be cast down, patiently bear every cross, laying all your sorrow on the Lord. Compelling yourself energetically to everything that is good, walk along

the narrow, holy path of virtue which will lead you to the Kingdom of Heaven.

'Remember that God has given us freedom and that he will
not take anyone to himself by force. You must display effort in
your will in order to receive the grace of the Holy Spirit in your.
heart.

'If God had not given us freedom, he would have destroyed
the way of faith and drawn everyone to himself by way of
enforced knowledge. Do not say, as some ignorant people do:
"Prove the existence of God to us and then we will believe."
There would be no faith if there was proof; there would be
enforced knowledge, and then there would be no way to salvation.

'However, when an act of faith is performed in a free heart,
then God gives such proofs of the truth of faith as are incomparably higher than scientific proofs.

'Always remember: you must make a freewill effort in life for
acquiring virtue and for communion with God in prayer. The
Lord will not take a soul to himself by force.

'Guard the pearl of faith, which is the way to bliss for us and
for the people close to your hearts.'

Father Zosima had a friend in the monastery, Father Irenaeus, an archimandrite, a man of lofty spiritual life.

One day he came to Father Zosima and said: 'Father
Zosima, my friend, I have come to you to bid you farewell and
to confess to you. Confess me in detail, thoroughly, for I want to
die tomorrow. I shall go down to the early Mass, take communion, and then I shall die.'

'What are you saying, Father Irenaeus?' said Father Zosima,
'You are still not old, you're healthy, so what are these thoughts
that have come over you?' 'No, I'm telling the truth, I shall die
tomorrow. You must come to my help and be my defender in
the second coming.' 'Live a little longer, many people need
you.' 'No, I shall die tomorrow, but you will live and be a
mentor, a consoler, a model of prayer for suffering, sinful,
lonely people, you will be a father to orphans, cripples, boys
and babes-in-arms. The Queen of Heaven has appointed you to
this ministry to men.' 'Irenaeus my dear friend . . .' 'Listen to

what I say, and confess me for the last time.'

A moving confession and leave-taking took place between the two friends. But all the same Father Zosima was not entirely convinced that Father Irenaeus would give up his soul to God the next day. Perhaps soon, but not the next day.

In the morning, passing the cell of his friend, archimandrite Irenaeus, on his way to his duties, Father Zosima caught sight of the novice who waited on him, and with a feeling of deep love for his friend he said: 'Give my friend archimandrite Irenaeus a greeting from me.' 'Give him your greeting!' said the novice in confusion. 'Your friend is already laid out on the table. He took communion at the early Mass, came back, and I began to put on the samovar. I went into his cell to tell him his tea was ready, and the blessed man was already lying there on his bed, with his arms folded on his chest.'

The Lord revealed many wonderful and helpful things to his chosen one, Father Zosima, seeing his steadfast faith in the providence of God, without which even faith in God is insulting.

If someone believes in God, then he must believe without any doubt that all the circumstances of life are accomplished according to the will of God, or with God being pleased to permit them.

The elder often used to repeat: 'No hair will fall from a head unless it is the will of God.' He said that we must be cheerful, and that we greatly offend the will of the Lord when, because of the afflictions and sorrows which befall us, we fall into depression, grumbling, despair, disproportionate grief and hardened insensitivity.

These horrors are the threshold of the fiery Gehenna. The downcast soul is already engulfed in a blazing fire worse than that of Gehenna, there is no longer any feeling left in it, except for one sharp, painful feeling which kills and burns everything. Misfortunes and sorrows are sent us by Providence to test us, and to strengthen us for the life of spiritual heroism.

The greatest feat is to endure without grumbling to the end of one's days all that is sent down upon us in this vale of tears. 'But he that endureth to the end shall be saved' (Matt. 10.22).

You should never ascribe to yourself painful incidents which you or those close to you experience. No, all this is not from you, but is sent down upon you, as a cross to bear. So bear it with good humour, inspired by radiant hope and firm faith that there 'where there is neither disease, nor sorrow, nor lamentation,' there in life eternal, the affliction you have borne here with hope and endurance will give you and those close to you such joy and such closeness to perfect Love and Truth as man cannot begin to imagine. If you bear affliction with endurance, you witness by doing so to your faithfulness to Christ, your devotion to the Saviour and your love to the One who rose from the dead and is calling us all to himself.

Let us not love that which does not last. Every earthly happiness is short-lived and ends in death. Let us always strive above all towards the eternal and be mindful of eternal life, and most of all let us be mindful of our end in the holy words of the Gospel: 'As I find, so shall I judge.'

The elder had one more dear friend in the St Sergius monastery, the blessed Nicholas. He was a wonderful person. His full name was Nicholas Alexandrovich Ivansen. His father's name was Oscar. He had changed his name and adopted Orthodoxy. His mother's name was Natalya. The blessed Nicholas was a soldier by profession, but he did not keep his health for long. He bore a heavy cross of illness; once he had fallen ill he did not rise from his bed for forty years. At first he lay in a private flat, but afterwards he was moved into the monastery almshouse. His parents had died and there was no-one to look after him, he was a stranger to everyone. With courage he endured and prayed.

For his exceptional endurance and humility, the Lord endowed him with prescience. Father Zosima began to go to see him often and the blessed man became very fond of him.

Ten years before the revolution, Nicholas predicted that the Tsar would be overthrown, that the St Sergius Monastery would be closed and all the monks driven away, and that they would live in private flats.

He even told Father Zosima his future place of residence: 'You will live in Moscow and you will be given the ruined daughter church of a monastery. You will live with your spiritual children. In Moscow you will be made an archimandrite. I tell you, be ready to go clean away from the monastery.'

No-one believed him at that time, and his words seemed strange and absurd to everyone.

One day Nicholas healed Father Zosima's sister Maria, who suffered from blindness. For ten years the old lady had not looked on God's earth. The blessed man directed that her eyes be anointed with oil from the lamp that was burning before his icon, and Maria the servant of God recovered her sight and lived for another ten years as a sighted person.

One day when Father Zosima was sitting with his friend, a young man came to see him. The blessed man seized his fur cap and said: 'I shan't give it up, it's not your cap. Yours is lying behind the train carriage.' When he left the blessed man, Father Zosima asked him to disclose what he had done with his cap. 'This is what I did,' replied the young man. 'When I got out of the carriage, I saw a drunk lying there, with a new cap lying beside him. I took it for myself and threw my old one behind the carriage. And now the blessed man has exposed me; clearly everything is known to him.'

In truth he was a wonderful servant of God.

Several times in succession angels brought him Communion, coming to him in the guise of monks, with the abbot at their head, who confessed him. The monks sang wonderfully. They came to him by night. The blessed Nicholas did not realise that this was a heavenly favour shown to him, but took the angels for monks and thought: 'This is how well the abbot and the brothers behave to me; they have no time during the day, so they come by night on holy days and comfort me in my great suffering.'

Father Zosima did not know about this, and when he learnt from the brothers that Nicholas was lying seriously ill in the monastery almshouse and that for more than thirty years no-one had administered Christ's Holy Sacrament to him, he went to give him Communion and confess him. The blessed Nicholas thanked him and said: 'I am so glad that on all the great feast-days the abbot and the brothers give me Communion,' and he told him everything.

Father Zosima stored up the blessed man's words in his

heart, but he did not say anything to him, and only after his death did he learn of the wonderful miracle shown to this suffering soul, which had borne its cross with great endurance.

The gift of prescience was given to Father Zosima.

This is a story told by one of the elder's spiritual daughters: 'I first saw the elder in Sergievo Posad.* He was in his cell, surrounded by various suffering people. He was giving them tea to drink, but there were not enough teaspoons. I remembered that I still had a few silver teaspoons left from my father, and thought that the next time I came to the elder I would bring the teaspoons and present them to him. Scarcely had this thought passed through my head than the elder looked at me affectionately and said: "A few – but I won't take even one silver teaspoon, a monk has no need of silver teaspoons." I was amazed at the elder's intuition.'

He could have said nothing; he knew everything, past and future.

One old priest went to him for confession and had great difficulty in revealing to him everything that was worrying him. The elder began to enumerate his sins to him and said: 'That is the number and kind of sins that I have, and you have just the same ones, haven't you, so repent and I will give you absolution from them.'

The priest was astonished. The elder had purposely enumerated all his sins, and in order to conceal his prescience had said: 'These are the kind of sins I have.'

This priest told me about this himself.

Once Father Zosima said: 'I asked the Lord to come into me, so that I would not dare to say anything myself, but would say only what the Lord ordered me to say. Sometimes I have a feeling of reverential terror inside myself when I sense the power and the voice of God. I know that sometimes my words cause people pain, and sometimes God consoles them by my words, but I am obliged to say to them what God inspires me to say. Now I say nothing of my own, nothing at all.' The word of God will always come to pass, because he is Truth and Life.

One day the elder put into his mouth quite a large silver cross

* The old name for Zagorsk. (Translator's note.)

and appealed to the Lord in prayer: 'O Lord, Lord, come into me, come into me in your cross. Let this cross melt in my mouth and I will swallow it, and let your cross live in me . . .' The cross melted and the elder swallowed it, like living water, holy and blessed.

Before the dispersal of the monastery, the elder had once more to endure many hard things from his brothers.

Father Zosima forewarned the abbot, Father Kronits, saying to him: 'St Sergius appeared to me and said: "You will be dispersed and you will live in private flats." I will live for a time with a spiritual daughter in Pereyaslavka, and you, Father Kronits, will live just over two miles from Khotkov.'

Despite the approaching danger, the monks continued not to live as befits monks. Tears of blood wrung the heart of the spiritual leader Father Zosima when he looked at their lives.

One day, on one of the great feasts, there was a ceremonial service in the cathedral. Suddenly the Queen of Heaven came out of the Royal Gates, surrounded by four great martyrs, and looked upon all the monks of the monastery praying in the church. But the Most Pure Lady looked upon them with sad eyes, and said: 'There are no monks here, except for those three or four,' and she pointed with her hand to the elder Zosima and another three monks. The great martyrs and the Most Pure and Ever Virgin Mary went into the sanctuary and disappeared.

The monastic habit, the tonsure, it is not all this which makes a man a monk. He who enters on this path must imitate the life of the angels. He must live in a state of unceasing prayer, of love to all men, he must practise all the virtues, be in a state of humility, considering himself to be nothing, he must judge no-one and must try with all his strength, and the help of God, to bring about the salvation of those near him.

The elder Zosima did not cease to remind people of eternity, he could not indifferently pass by souls perishing from unbelief. He felt pity for all of them. You do not pass by a river in which poor, irresponsible children are drowning. Every one of us would try to pull the children out and save them to live longer; we would return them to their parents so that they might grow up and bring joy to others. How then can one pass by godless sinners or heretics who are drowning in the river of delusions and drowning for all eternity, when the deeps of hell will swallow them for evermore?

Sometimes the elder would say to unbelievers: 'Why have you forgotten, don't you know God, don't you see God? Believers see God much more brightly than you see the sun and the sky. But they see with their hearts. Well, you all know and see me, sinful Zosima, so at least be mindful of me and my love for God, and I will prostrate myself before the Lord and beseech him for you. O poor people, people who have taken leave of your senses, who has done you this harm? I think it is those who, bearing the outward image of a Christian, have spurned its powers; those who, calling themselves Christians, do not fulfil the fundamental commandment of love to one's neighbour. You see, the aim of the Christian life consists of possessing the Holy Spirit within oneself, so that the nature of man, changed by this Spirit, as though all enlightened and strengthened, may serve its neighbours in a feat of pure love in models of the loftiest wisdom and beauty. As for how to acquire this treasure of the King of Heaven in our hearts, the saints teach us this by their lives and by their divinely-inspired writings.'

CHAPTER 4

The Closure of the Monastery

The elder's love for St Sergius, as I have already written, was especially deep; it was as though he lived by his thoughts and desires, penetrating to the depths of the saint's heart.

The elder did not wish to be separated from the place where his beloved saint had performed his great spiritual feat, but the saint himself said to him: 'I shall go away, and you will go away too, Zosima,' and he showed him the flat where he would settle after the dispersal of the Monastery.

The elder asked: 'What about the relics?' To this St Sergius replied: 'My spirit will depart, but my relics will remain to be desecrated.'

Little by little, Father Zosima resigned himself to this.

All the brothers were evicted, and he remained alone, according to the words of Father Barnabas.

Several men arrived from the administration and began to demand that the elder should abandon his cell immediately. 'Get out of the monastery.' 'No, I will not go now,' said the elder. 'We'll throw you out, what is all this?' they shouted angrily at him.

The elder took a cross and outlined, or rather enclosed, his room with it, saying: 'Go on and try then, dare to cross this line which I have drawn around my cell, just try it and at once you will drop dead.'

'What kind of an old man is this?' the new arrivals began to say in embarrassment. The power of the elder's words was so great that none of them dared to cross the line beyond which Father Zosima had forbidden them to pass. It was really very strange; armed, healthy young men were filled with fear and said: 'Let us leave this old man, he will go away by himself.' They stood there for a while and then dispersed.

The elder prayed for everyone until the last minute, begging the Saint to forgive all those who had broken the commandment of God.

He asked for blessing for all the brothers who had dispersed to private flats. Once again he begged the Saint that when it pleased the Queen of Heaven, she might open her monastery so that many monks could be saved there. He remembered the vision of St Sergius, who one day saw a flock of birds, and it was revealed to him that his disciples would increase so greatly that it would be difficult to count them.

At last Father Zosima's time came too, and he was the last to leave the Holy Trinity Monastery of the Saint and God-bearer, our Father Sergius, abbot of Radonezh. When the Holy Trinity Monastery of St Sergius was closed, the superior of the monastery turned to the elder in great sorrow with the question: 'Where am I to settle now?'

The elder felt sorry for the superior and said: 'Go where the Saint gave me his blessing for you to go, it will be a good place for you. I will follow my nose.'

Father Zosima went to Moscow. He arrived at the Sukharev tower, near which there was a chapel. The monk who was on duty in the chapel asked him: 'Where are you from, old man of God?' 'From a destroyed hermitage,' was the humble reply. 'Stay with us for the night.' 'No,' replied the elder, 'I am afraid that you will all be arrested,' and he went away. And in fact that night everyone in the chapel was arrested.

The elder, however, moved to the Serbsky daughter church of the monastery, to his spiritual son, Father Seraphim B. At that time E.G.P. was staying as a guest of Father Seraphim. When she learnt that the elder had nowhere to live, she invited him to her house.

So it was that our long-suffering exile travelled to Tver region. The Savvinsky daughter church in the yard of their flat was not yet closed, and the elder sometimes officiated there.

After a little while the people sensed the grace that dwelt in the elder and began to come to him in his cell. But by no means all of them were admitted to him by the lady of the house. In the church, however, the crowd jostled round him, and he consoled, encouraged and drove out demons.

A grief-stricken person had only to talk to the elder for a few minutes and suddenly all his depression and grief would vanish, and tranquillity would be established in his heart; his mind saw God, and such a good, childishly clear and pure feeling came over his heart, as it does on Easter night to a happy child, surrounded by the love of all those near and dear to him, a child who has not tasted grief, who has not known passions and sins. The elder seemed to resurrect and renew the soul that turned to him.

It is impossible to describe the elder's prescience. He saw far ahead into the life of every man. He foretold the imminent death of some people, while to others, like a tender, solicitous mother, he said nothing, but prepared them to pass into eternity.

More than once we heard these words from the elder: 'Sometimes I say something I didn't at all expect to say, which surprises myself. I have yielded my lips, my heart and my soul to our Saviour and Lord Jesus Christ, and I say and do what he inspires. I do not possess my own words or my own will.'

One day an old woman came to the elder with a young relative, a healthy, blooming girl. Suddenly the elder said to the girl: 'Tomorrow take the Holy Sacrament of Christ and I will confess you. But now go and wash my stairs. In fact they are almost clean, but I am telling you to do it so that on every step you will remember your sins and repent, and when you dry them, remember all the stages of the soul through purgatory.'

When the girl had gone out to wash the stairs, her relative asked the elder in surprise: 'Why must she take Communion* tomorrow? It isn't a fast, is it? She has not prepared, her health is blooming, must she even prepare for the fast by fasting?' 'Tomorrow you will understand why she must not put off taking Communion. Come to me after early Mass and we will have a talk.'

When the girl had washed the stairs, the elder confessed her, gave her absolution of her sins for her whole life, and gazed at

---

* Orthodox believers hear Mass regularly, but make their Communion infrequently and with strenuous preparation. (Translator's note.)

her with great affection and fatherly love. He gave them both a drink of tea and bade them farewell.

Next day the girl took Communion and arrived home feeling fine and full of joy. Her relative had been baking pies, and went to put on the samovar. The girl sat down on a chair and apparently fell asleep. The Lord took her soul painlessly, in a moment. Stunned by her death, the old woman ran to the elder, and found him at prayer for the late-lamented girl. He consoled the old woman: 'Now, what are you upset about? I knew that the Lord would take her, you see, and that is why I gave her my blessing to take Communion in haste.' He said much more, consoling the old woman, who was astounded by the sudden death.

One day, when the priest was taking a service in church, a lady who had never met him came to the service, and, when she encountered this aged and amazingly thin man, thought: 'Well, what sort of a monk is this? How is he to attract the people into church? He will drive out all those who come.' Suddenly, instead of going in to the altar, the elder began to force his way through the crowd to this lady and said to her: 'Olga, don't be afraid, I won't drive anyone out.' Astounded by his spiritual penetration the lady, whose name was in fact Olga, fell at the elder's feet, begging his forgiveness for her thoughts, and afterwards always came to him for advice.

A certain nun, sitting at table with the priest, conjectured: 'If I were clever, things would be quite different, I would please the Lord better than I do now, when I am so uneducated.' The elder looked at her and said: 'The Lord does not need learned people, he needs only love.'

One woman, a servant of God, had nowhere to relax, neither with friends nor relatives, but the priest said: 'Don't grieve, every shrub is allowed to rest for the night.' And, to the lonely woman's surprise, some people she hardly knew began to beg her to go to relax in the country with them.

One day the elder invited his spiritual children to dinner and sat down at table with them, but then suddenly stood up and said: 'There is my Pelageya, how she is repenting, how she is begging me to absolve her sins, she is even weeping. Wait, children, forget your meal, pray with me.'

The elder went to the icon corner, read a prayer of absolution and blessed his repentant spiritual daughter. 'Where is it that she is repenting now, father?' 'She is in the north now. When she arrives here, I will ask her about her repentance. Make a note of the day and the hour.' Sure enough, Pelageya arrived in her homeland within six months and told the elder how deeply she had repented and wept and begged the elder to absolve her at exactly the day and the hour when the elder had absolved her of her sins.

There was another case with two ladies. They were on their way to the elder's cell and one of them was repenting of her sins every step of the way: 'O Lord, how sinful I am, there is this and that that I have done wrongly, someone I have judged, forgive me, O Lord . . .' and her heart and mind as it were fell at the feet of the Lord, '. . . forgive me, O Lord, and give me strength not to offend you any more, forgive me, O Lord.' In her mind she went over her whole life and all the time she kept on repenting.

The other woman, however, was placid as she walked to the elder. 'I shall arrive, go to confession, say that I am guilty of everything, tomorrow I shall take Communion, but now as I walk along the road I shall think over what kind of material I shall buy for my daughter's dress, and what kind of style to choose for her, that will suit her face . . .' These and similar worldly thoughts occupied the heart and mind of the second lady.

They entered Father Zosima's cell together. Addressing the first, the elder said: 'Kneel down, I will absolve you of your sins at once.' 'How can you, father, I haven't told you them yet, have I?' 'You don't have to tell them, you told them to the Lord all the time, you were repenting to him the whole way, and I heard everything, so that now I absolve you, and give you my blessing to take Communion tomorrow.'

'But you,' he addressed the other lady after a few moments, 'you go and buy the material for your daughter's dress, choose the style, sew it, do as you planned. But when your soul comes to repentance, come to confession. I will not confess you now.'

There were also two girl students who came to the elder's cell who experienced the considerable power of Father Zosima's prescience at work on them. They had heard a lot from others about the remarkable priest and his unusual good sense, and had decided to ask him about everything, whatever interested and worried them. They decided to set forth right away all the problems of life they did not understand. They wrote down the most varied questions, social, aesthetic, philosophical, family problems and simply psychological difficulties. One student had almost forty of these questions, and the other had fifteen.

They arrived: the elder was busy, there were many people to see him.

'Wait a little, children, sit over there in the corner, I must attend to them first, they have come from a long way away.'

The students waited and waited. At length they had no patience to wait any longer. Suddenly the elder glanced at them: 'Why are you in a hurry? Well, you first, Lyubov, take out your forty questions then, find a pencil and write.' 'I'll read them to you at once, father.' 'There's no need to read them, just write down the answers.' And the elder gave answers to all the forty questions, not omitting one, and all the answers were exhaustive. 'And now you, Elizabeth, take out your fifteen puzzles.' And again, without reading them or asking them what they wanted to know from him, he gave answers in the order in which the questions were written down.

'And now you must go. Think over what I have said to you. May the Lord bless you, but suffering people are coming to me, I have no time today, come again another time.'

All their lives these two students were deeply devoted to the elder. One of them died of consumption at just over forty years of age, and on her death-bed she saw the elder; he came to her and blessed her. He was alive as he stood by her bed. When she was in exile, the elder appeared to her in a dream, performed the ceremony of taking the veil and gave her the name Anastasia, although her life had turned out in such a way that it was difficult to think of taking monastic vows.

Several times the elder appointed the time of a person's death, or foretold it.

The elder had a certain spiritual daughter, a merchant's

wife, a little old woman called Reshetnikova. She often visited the elder. Then one day she came to the elder in tears. 'I am exhausted,' she said, 'because of my son Paul; he has let himself go completely and has fallen into grave sins. He does not honour God, does not go to church, does not take the sacraments, offends his parents, drinks, smokes and goes boozing with various women. I have spoken to him, restrained him, begged him, admonished him. He jeers at me and carries on doing as he wants. I no longer sleep at nights, my eyes are never dry. I am so sorry for my son; my beloved son is perishing, the son of my heart is perishing. Earthly life flies past like a dream, and what has he earned there in the eternal life? You may believe or not believe, but every man will have to give the Lord an answer for his every deed, for his every action, and my dear Paul has begun to swear in obscene, abusive bad language, he constantly uses bad words. Why, even Father Aristocles, who is now dead, said that there is no greater offence for the Lord and the Queen of Heaven than if someone swears with this bad language – by this he offends the Lord and the Queen of Heaven and Mother Earth and his own mother. But my Paul . . .' and the old woman burst into bitter tears.

The elder felt sorry for the suffering woman, he consoled her and gave her advice, but not to any great advantage. Paul rode roughshod over them, holding them of no account, and continued his outrageous way of life.

One day the mother brought her son to Father Zosima almost by force. He was rude to the elder and continued to live just as he wanted, gratifying all the desires of the flesh. The elder prayed for Paul, attempting to awaken in him at least a spark of repentance, but he did not reform. His attitude to the priesthood was one of coarse mockery and contempt, and he did not want to hear anything spiritual or holy.

One day the elder met Paul in the street and began to speak to him with affection and heartfelt consideration. The young man rudely cut him short and with some gibe thrust a rouble at him. The elder immediately gave this rouble away to the poor and prayed to the Lord that he would accept even this offering, though it was so coldly given, and for the sake of it would save the soul of a young man who had lost his way and drowned in his sins.

'O Lord, O Queen of Heaven, reveal to me what must be done so that Paul's soul will not perish, so that he will repent and inherit eternal life.' More than once he petitioned for him at the throne of God, and the Lord revealed to the elder that Paul would repent and be saved only when he appointed imminent death for him, in a fixed month and on a fixed date. The elder felt sorry for the mother and prayed to God that perhaps there might be some other way to reform Paul. Again the answer was the same: 'There is no other way for him, talk to his mother, appoint the time of his death.'

Once again the old mother came to the elder and, bursting into tears, told him about her son's outrages.

'Mother,' the elder said boldly to her, 'If you want, in order that your son may be saved, give me your agreement to appoint his death within a year. Then he will come to his senses, fall ill, change his mind, repent, take the Holy Sacrament of Christ and die a Christian. Otherwise he will not come to God and his soul will perish for ever. Do you agree or not? Tell me.'

For a long time the old woman would not agree, but time continued to pass and Paul grew worse and worse, and at length the mother herself came to the elder and began to beg him to treat her son as God directed and, if necessary, to appoint his death. Let him appoint it, provided that the soul of her beloved son might be saved.

'Well then, sister, tell your son that I appoint his death in exactly a year's time, on such-and-such a month and date, at such-and-such an hour. Let him repent and prepare for eternity.'

The old woman began to cry, but no longer with tears of despair but with profound tears of faith, beginning to see clearly into the distance, into eternity.

The mother spoke to her son, who paid not the slightest attention to her words.

But time passed, the time for the fulfilment of Father Zosima's words drew near, and the young, blooming Paul fell ill with typhus and took to his death-bed. A few days later he came to the point of repentance and a priest was summoned from the Novodevichy Monastery. The dying man made his confession, took Communion, took his leave of everyone, and passed into eternity as peacefully and calmly as a child, having asked forgiveness of everyone, strengthened in faith, hope and love.

The astounded mother immediately went to the elder to tell him of her son's death. On entering the cell, she was extremely surprised to find the elder ending a requiem for her late son Paul.

'Now you see, sister, how great is the grace of God. Your son has entered the Kingdom of Heaven. His rouble given to the poor was not wasted. The Lord gave him an easy, blessed end. But he forgot to confess his sin to a priest and I absolved him in his absence. Well, don't grieve now, but rejoice and prepare yourself for the heavenly dwelling-place. Your hour is also very close.'

Paul died at the very month, day and hour which Father Zosima had appointed for his death.

The elder Zosima taught his spiritual children to respect and love the Most Holy Trinity.

God is One, but triune, and this mystery of the Holy Trinity is the greatest Love, Wisdom and Truth. It is impossible to think of and sense God outside the Trinity. God is the Trinity.

Father Zosima noticed and raised up reverentially in his heart to God everything that reminded him of the Trinity. If it happened simply that three men met together, he would at once think of the Holy Trinity and say: 'Good, it is good for three people to eat a meal and talk of the Deity together in honour of the Holy Trinity.'

If a lamp was burning, the elder would say: 'There is a flame flickering; it can burn because there is a wick, oil and fire. Three things make one – the burning of the lamp.'

The elder gave one of his spiritual daughters his blessing to draw the Old Testament model of the Holy Trinity. It is portrayed thus: Abraham is receiving three pilgrims in the form of angels and serving them. The New Testament Holy Trinity is portrayed on icons as God the Father in the form of an Elder,

God the Son our Lord and Saviour Jesus Christ, and the Holy Spirit in the form of a dove.

The elder did not part with the icon of the Holy Trinity and always kept it in his cell. After his death this icon accompanied him into both the church and the grave.

'Every Christian should come to know and love the Holy Trinity,' the elder exhorted his children. 'My hope is the Father, my refuge is the Son, my protection is the Holy Spirit. Most Holy Trinity, have mercy on us; O Lord, cleanse us from our sins, Master, forgive our lawlessness, Holy Spirit, visit us and heal our sickness, for the sake of your name. "Lord, have mercy" – three times. Change and transform me from every kind of evil to virtue. May the one, unchanging and inexpressible Trinity enlighten me by your light.

'It is necessary for every Christian to know the services of the Holy Trinity. One must study the church services and the church statutes, because the beauty and profundity of Christian worship is higher than that of angels, it is the link between earth and heaven. It is a choir of angels and men striving towards the union of their hearts with God, and of their wills with the will of God.

'One should see to it that one's soul is pure, that it is entirely yielded to God. One must not lie, be cunning, or be depressed. One must strictly differentiate the various kinds of lies: by thought, by language, by word, by deed, by life, and one must remember that the devil is the father of lies, and that whoever lies makes the devil his father.'

The elder recounted, and even dictated, one incident, moving in its profound content, which occurred with a certain young man who was completely unacquainted with falsehood, distinguished by his child-like truthfulness. Here is depicted the soul of a pure, upright man with a childishly strong and simple faith, uneducated, but possessing a pure soul and will, striving towards God, a soul which made him a little less than the angels. He was indeed growing wise, capable of seeing the heavenly as well as the earthly.

This incident took place in Russia, in the remote depths of the country, at a distance of several hundred miles from the nearest village.

There lived a peasant orphan, completely illiterate, but very hard-working; he was always working, and spent not a moment in idleness. His soul was as pure as crystal. He always listened to his conscience in every matter. His conscience was righteous, not feeble, but truly righteous, sensitive and strict. In his simple way, he never offended it by disobedience, and so he always heard its voice. If a man disobeys his conscience once, twice or more, then he stops hearing it.

This simple man observed fasts, and was satisfied with very little. He was always cheerful and full of the joy of life, and never judged anyone, considering himself to be worse and lower than everyone else.

One day he heard from a pilgrim that in order to be saved, one must take up one's cross and follow Christ. Our simpleton had never once been in church as an adult, since it was very far away from his little hamlet. He had been baptised in church as a baby, but he did not remember it. 'You must take up your cross and follow Christ' – our simple young man understood these words literally.

He ordered an enormous wooden cross and resolved to take it and follow Christ. His pure soul yearned towards God, his heart thirsted for salvation, but how was he to follow? Where? In what way? Where was Christ? There was the cross, but where should he carry it?

The simple man left all his few possessions, and his work, hoisted his cross onto his shoulder, and set off. He went, as the saying goes, following his nose. He walked for a long, long time and at last, in a dense forest, he ran across a male monastery. He knocked at the gates. 'Who are you?' asked the gate-keeper in surprise, 'where are you going with your cross?'

'Well, here I am, carrying my cross, but I don't know how to get to Christ; won't you point out the way to me?'

'Here's a real crank, I'll go and tell the abbot.' The monk went off and told the abbot, who was surprised and ordered the simpleton to be brought to him. 'But he won't come, he keeps refusing to leave his cross, and he can't come into your cell with his cross, it is much too big.' The abbot went out himself to the simpleton. He talked to him, and saw that he was a man of God.

'Well, if you like, we will help you to reach Christ, we are also going to Him.' 'Then where are your crosses?' asked the new-comer, 'you know, the Lord will not accept you without a cross.' 'They are in us, we carry them inside ourselves,' said the abbot.

'How can that be?' said the newcomer in surprise. 'You will see for yourself how. But for the time being I give you my con-sent to remain here, and you will have a duty – tidying up in the church. Take your cross and bring it down there, into the church.'

The simpleton entered the church with trepidation and began to tidy up. He raised his head, and froze. Up above him, right over the altar, a large wooden cross had been made, and on it the Lord was portrayed, full-length, crucified. Our simple-ton had never seen anything like it before. He stared at it: nails had been driven into the hands and feet, and they were bleed-ing. On his breast there was also blood and a wound. His head also was completely covered in blood, his face was swollen and beaten. Who was he? Who was he? Who are you, man? You also bore your cross and were not parted from it. But how is it that you are still hanging on it? The blood rushed to the simpleton's heart. He felt such love and pity for the Sufferer, that it seemed he would give up his life if only he could serve the Sufferer and help him.

'But how can you hang there all the time without food? Come down, come down from your cross, and I will feed you.' On his knees, the simple man lifted up his hands and prayed and prayed without stopping. 'Come down, come to me, teach me how and where I must carry my cross. Perhaps I too must be crucified on it?'

Thus he prayed to the Crucified One for several days and nights with all his heart, and fell down before him, and was soaked through with his own tears. And the Crucified Lord, hearing the prayers raised up to him from a full heart, came· down from the cross, and taught the simpleton how he should bear his cross in order to come into the Kingdom of Heaven. No one can be saved without his cross.

The Lord revealed to the simpleton the mystery of the Triune God, the mystery of the love of the Holy Trinity, the Father, the Son and the Holy Spirit. 'I am the Son of the Heavenly Father and have redeemed the human race with my cross. No-one will enter the Kingdom of Heaven without his cross. No-one will receive the grace of the Holy Spirit in his heart without his cross. You need only to join your cross with the cross of Golgotha, and to wind around it, like roses, deeds of charity.'

The simpleton listened to everything and received the Holy Spirit in his heart, and the Lord revealed to him that within a few days he would depart into the Kingdom of Heaven. The simpleton began joyfully to prepare for death, praising ceaselessly and thanking God for everything. He also revealed to the abbot the hour of his end. The abbot shed a few tears and begged him to say a few prayers before the Lord for him also. With the whole of his pure heart the simpleton began to intercede for the abbot with the Saviour: 'Take him into the Kingdom of Heaven also, release him from this temporal life.' 'But why should he be taken, he is not yet ready.' 'O, take him for the sake of the favour he did to me when he gave me a double portion of bread, of which I brought half to you. Do a favour to him, for the sake of the favour he did. Take him into the Kingdom of Heaven.

'O Lord, our God, you are our Saviour, crucified for us, answer my prayer, do not deprive him either of your ineffable grace and joy.'

The Lord heard the prayers of the simpleton and revealed to him the hour of the abbot's death, and the simpleton disclosed to him the hour of his end. The abbot began to prepare for his translation into eternity.

At the appointed day and hour the simpleton passed away to the Lord, and two weeks later at the appointed day and hour the abbot passed away to the Lord.

CHAPTER 5

Teaching on Prayer

Father Zosima had a special love for the Queen of Heaven. He seemed to be always standing before her.

The elder commanded his children to address themselves to her constantly, as to their Mother Superior, and to ask for her blessing in all their actions. 'Do not begin to do anything, my children, without the blessing of the Queen of Heaven. When you have finished the matter, thank her again, Our Lady Swift to Hear and to help us in all good matters.'

The elder considered it essential to light the lamps before the icons of the Queen of Heaven. If someone fell ill, he must be anointed with oil which had burned before the miracle-working icon of the Mother of God, and this would bring healing for the soul and body of the sick person. The elder had two miracle-working icons of the Queen of Heaven in his cell: Our Lady of Vladimir and Our Lady of Kazan. Many miracles were performed thanks to these icons, many sick people received healing. Today one of them, Our Lady of Vladimir, is in the possession of a spiritual daughter of the elder.

When the elder turned to the Queen of Heaven in prayer, he spoke to her as though she were alive and he could see her right there in his cell. And in fact, the Queen of Heaven was always with him, and the entire inner and outward life of the elder passed under her protection. And he exhorted all his spiritual children to say daily, every hour of the twenty-four: 'O Hail, Mother of God and Virgin,'* (the whole prayer to the end) and to beg for the blessing of the Ever Virgin Mary on every hour of their lives and on the lives of those near to them.

* The full text of the prayer is: 'Hail, Mother of God and Virgin, Mary full of grace, the Lord is with thee. Blessed art thou among women and blessed is the fruit of thy womb, for thou hast given birth to the Saviour of our souls.' (Translator's note.)

The elder rejoiced if any of his spiritual children fulfilled the Rule of the Mother of God, saying the 'O Hail, Mother of God and Virgin . . .' one hundred and fifty times a day.

The Queen of Heaven herself had given this Rule, but everyone had forgotten it, they had forgotten about obedience to Our Lady Who Shows the Way, the Joy Above All Joys.

St Seraphim had reminded people of this Rule, making them walk along the ditch which encircled the Convent of Diveevo saying the prayer 'O Hail, Mother of God and Virgin' one hundred and fifty times. He instructed his spiritual children to fulfil this Rule.

In St Seraphim's cell was found a strange little book with descriptions of miracles which had taken place with people who performed this miracle-working Rule, repeating one hundred and fifty times the joyful news of the Archangel to the Queen of Heaven.

There were priests close to the elder who always fulfilled the Rule of the Mother of God. One of them was O. D. Kryuchkov, who had a burning love for the Kingdom of Heaven and was striving to enter it. He was inspired with his love for God and for his spiritual children, and taught them not to be tied to earth but to prepare boldly for eternal life, abiding always with the Queen of Heaven.

Another priest, Father Alexander Gumanovsky (whose monastic name was Daniel), was gentle and quiet, completely buried in his love for the Queen of Heaven. His whole life was constant servitude to the Ever Virgin Mary; all his spiritual children repeated one hundred and fifty prayers daily to the Mother of God, and some of them had been favoured with a passage into eternal life, offering up the good news of the Archangel to her who is more honoured than the cherubim and incomparably more glorious than the seraphim.

Both these elders died in exile.

Here is an extract from a letter of that most gentle man, Father Alexander Gumanovsky, who because of his love for the Queen of Heaven was nicknamed 'the Mother of God's elder' by one of his spiritual children.

'. . . I forgot to give you a piece of advice vital for salvation.

Say the "O Hail, Mother of God and Virgin" one hundred and fifty times, and this prayer will save you. This Rule was given by the Mother of God herself in about the eighth century, and at one time all Christians fulfilled it. We Orthodox have forgotten about it, and St Seraphim has reminded us of this Rule. In my hands I have a handwritten book from the cell of St Seraphim, containing a description of the many miracles which took place through praying to the Mother of God and especially through saying one hundred and fifty times the "O Hail, Mother of God and Virgin." If, being unaccustomed to it, it is difficult to master one hundred and fifty repetitions daily, say it fifty times at first. After every ten repetitions say the "Our Father" once and "Open unto us the doors of thy loving-kindness"*. Whoever he spoke to about this miracle-working Rule remained grateful to him . . .'

The elder Zosima greatly valued and loved Bishop Seraphim Zvezdinsky and always spoke of him as 'that saintly Bishop.' Bishop Seraphim Zvezdinsky performed the Rule of the Mother of God every day, and when he performed it he prayed for the whole world, embracing in this rule the whole life of the Queen of Heaven.

He gave one of his spiritual children the task of copying a plan in which he included his prayer to the Ever Virgin Mary. Here it is:

First decade: Let us remember the birth of the Mother of God – pray for mothers, fathers and children.

Second decade: Let us remember the feast of the Presentation of the Blessed Virgin and Mother of God – let us pray for those who have lost their way and fallen away from the church.

Third decade: Let us remember the Annunciation of the Blessed Mother of God – let us pray for the soothing of sorrows and the consolation of those who grieve.

Fourth decade: Let us remember the meeting of the Blessed Virgin with the righteous Elizabeth – let us pray for the reunion of the separated, for those whose dear ones or children are living

* The full text of the prayer is: 'Open unto us the door of thy loving-kindness, O blessed Mother of God; in that we set our hope on thee, we may not go astray; but through thee may we be delivered from all adversities, for thou art the salvation of all Christian people.' (Translator's note.)

away from them or missing.

Fifth decade: Let us remember the Birth of Christ – let us pray for the rebirth of souls, for new life in Christ.

Sixth decade: Let us remember the Feast of the Purification of the Lord, and the words uttered by St Simon: 'Yea, a sword shall pierce through thy own soul also' (Luke 2.35). Let us pray that the Mother of God will meet our souls at the hour of our death, and will contrive that we receive the Holy Sacrament with our last breath, and will lead our souls through the terrible torments.

Seventh decade: Let us remember the flight of the Mother of God with the God-child into Egypt. Let us pray that the Mother of God will help us avoid temptation in this life and deliver us from misfortunes.

Eighth decade: Let us remember the disappearance of the twelve-year-old boy Jesus in Jerusalem and the sorrow of the Mother of God on this account. Let us pray, begging the Mother of God for the constant repetition of the Jesus Prayer.

Ninth decade: Let us remember the miracle performed in Cana of Galilee, when the Lord turned water into wine at the words of the Mother of God: 'They have no wine (John 2.3). Let us ask the Mother of God for help in our affairs and deliverance from need.

Tenth decade: Let us remember the Mother of God standing at the cross of the Lord, when grief pierced through her heart like a sword. Let us pray to the Mother of God for the strengthening of our souls and the banishment of despondency.

Eleventh decade: Let us remember the Resurrection of Christ and ask the Mother of God in prayer to resurrect our souls and give us a new courage for spiritual feats.

Twelfth decade: Let us remember the Ascension of Christ, at which the Mother of God was present. Let us pray and ask the Queen of Heaven to raise up our souls from earthly and worldly amusements and direct them to striving for higher things.

Thirteenth decade: Let us remember the Upper Room and the descent of the Holy Spirit on the Apostles and the Mother of God. Let us pray: 'Create in me a clean heart, O God; and renew a right spirit within me. Cast me not away from thy presence; and take not thy holy spirit from me.'*

Fourteenth decade: Let us remember the Assumption of the Blessed Mother of God, and ask for a peaceful and serene end.

Fifteenth decade: Let us remember the glory of the Mother of God, with which the Lord crowned her after her removal from earth to heaven, and let us pray to the Queen of Heaven not to abandon the faithful who are on earth but to defend them from every evil, covering them with her honourable protecting veil.

After every decade Bishop Seraphim prayed his own prayers, which he revealed to no-one, so that only the Lord and the Queen of Heaven knew these prayers.

Some of those who performed the Rule of the Mother of God kept to Bishop Seraphim's plan, but did not know how to offer up their prayers. One of the nuns offered up the following prayers after every decade.

After the first decade: Our Lady, Blessed Mother of God, save and preserve your servants (names of parents, relatives and acquaintances), increase their faith and repentance, and when they die give them rest with the saints in your eternal glory.

After the second decade: Our Lady, Blessed Mother of God, save and preserve and unite or re-unite to the Holy Orthodox Church your servants who have lost their path and fallen away (names).

After the third decade: Our Lady, Blessed Mother of God, soothe our sorrows and send consolation to your servants who are grieving and ill (names).

After the fourth decade: Our Lady, Blessed Mother of God, unite your servants who are separated.

After the fifth decade: Our Lady, Blessed Mother of God, grant to us (me) who have been baptised in Christ, to be clothed in Christ.

After the sixth decade: Our Lady, Blessed Mother of God, let me receive the Holy Sacrament with my last breath, and lead my soul yourself through the terrible torments.

After the seventh decade: Our Lady, Blessed Mother of God, lead me not into temptation in this life and deliver me from

* Psalm 50.12–13 (Psalm 51.10–11 in the English Bible).

misfortunes.

After the eighth decade: Our Lady, Blessed Mother of God, grant to me the unceasing Jesus Prayer.

After the ninth decade: Our Lady, Blessed Mother of God, help me in all my affairs and deliver me from every need and sorrow.

After the tenth decade: Our Lady, Blessed Mother of God, help me in all my affairs and deliver me from every need and sorrow (*sic*; apparently a mistake in the Russian text. – Translator's note.)

After the eleventh decade: Our Lady, Blessed Mother of God, resurrect my soul and give me constant readiness for spiritual feats.

After the twelfth decade: Our Lady, Blessed Mother of God, deliver me from worldly thoughts and give me a mind and heart striving towards the salvation of my soul.

(Thirteenth prayer missing from Russian text – Translator's note.)

After the fourteenth decade: Our Lady, Blessed Mother of God, preserve me from every evil and cover me with your honourable protecting veil.

After the fifteenth decade: Our Lady, Blessed Mother of God, grant me a peaceful and serene end.

By no means everyone is able to perform the rule of the Mother of God according to the plan given by Bishop Seraphim Zvezdinsky, and almost everyone performs it as written down by Father Alexander Gumanovsky for his spiritual son in the letter I have quoted.

CHAPTER 6

Spiritual Children

The elder also greatly reverenced the Psalter and never forsook it. Every day he read three sections of the Psalter and when he was ill he consented to have someone read aloud to him. Every day he read the Gospels and the Psalter, and constantly repeated prayers.

He taught us, his spiritual children, to turn more frequently in prayer to St Sergius of Radonezh, the Miracle-Worker, whom he had seen more than once in a waking vision.

'I testify with a clear conscience,' the elder would say, 'that St Sergius stands at the Throne of God with arms uplifted and prays for everyone. Oh, if only you knew the power of his prayer and of his love for us, then you would turn to him every hour, asking for his help, protection and blessing for those for whom our hearts grieve, for our near and dear ones living here on this earth, and for those who are already beyond, in eternal life.'

The elder entrusted one of his spiritual daughters entirely to St Sergius:

'St Sergius our Lord and Father, abbot of Radonezh, gives you his blessing for constant prayer: take this rosary, as from his own hands.'

Often, when absolving her sins, he would say to her: 'It is not I who absolve your sins, but St Sergius who absolves them for you.'

In the elder's stole was sewn a piece of the relics of St Sergius.

The elder saw many miracles as he stood on duty at the shrine of the Saint's relics. He saw St John of Kronstadt* come up to the shrine and say: 'Father, St Sergius, my friend, I want to imitate you, to follow in your footsteps.' And we know that St

---

* Father John of Kronstadt (1829–1909) is revered as a saint, but not so far canonised. (Translator's note.)

71

Sergius heeded his request.

'Never forget, my children, the feats of St Sergius and of St Seraphim of Sarov the Miracle-Worker who imitated him. Both these saints were in especially close communion with the grace of the Mother of God. Our Lady appeared to them in waking visions, strengthened them and healed them. Let us then not forget her love to these saints, of whom Our Lady said: 'They are of our kin.' Let us run as often as possible to their protection, let us carefully memorise their lives. Let us learn their precepts by heart. And because of the prayers of her chosen ones, the Mother of God will not abandon us or those close to us.

'The saints loved God, and in God they loved all men.

'The whole world lies in evil, but the world itself is not evil.' ('World' means all the passions together.)

'We must lighten the lives of other people, especially suffering people, with deep, holy love. We must draw others to God as we ourselves draw close to heaven by our constant repentance. Our God is a God of love.

'Some people, who do not have God in their hearts, give the name love to things the complete opposite of love, namely, passion, egoistic affection, desire, and so on.

'"God is love." Christ prays for us thus: "Father, I will that they also, whom thou hast given me, be with me where I am; that they may behold my glory, which thou hast given me: for thou lovedst me before the foundation of the world.

'"O righteous Father, the world hath not known thee but I have known thee, and these have known that thou hast sent me. And I have declared unto them thy name, and will declare it: that the love wherewith thou hast loved me may be in them, and I in them" (John 17.24–26).

'Learn, my children, learn from St Sergius and St Seraphim, learn from them constant prayer and humble, Orthodox love to God and to your neighbour.'

The elder gave one of his spiritual children his consent to occupy herself with reading holy books and copying out extracts from them.*

---

* Under Soviet conditions, when few or no religious books are published,

She would come to the elder wanting to give him some help with his house-keeping, but he would not agree. 'No,' he would say, 'I can wash the dishes and sweep the floor better myself. You go and read, re-tell it to me and ask me what is not clear to you. Write down what I dictate to you. I give you my blessing, my child in spirit, to write my biography. I would not have wanted to pass on anything about myself to someone else. But my conscience commands me to do this, because it was not for an unworthy person like me that the Lord revealed his countless host of miracles and mercies, but for all of us who believe in his holy name, for all the children of the Orthodox Church. The Queen of Heaven commands me to dictate part of these divine favours which I have seen during the many years of my life, and I have chosen you and given you my consent to write all this down and pass it on to others, whom I shall not see with my own eyes in the flesh, but for whom I will pray, and whom I will see in the other, eternal life, which alone can be truly called life.

'The miracles which God has revealed to me were revealed not for one man, but for all, as I have already said, so that men would glorify the Triune Lord, so that they would fall down before the Queen of Heaven in all their needs and sorrows, and also in all their joys and successes.'

It is indispensable to glorify the name of the Lord. The apostles and saints performed miracles in the name of the Lord. The name of the Lord is the strongest weapon against the Evil One, against all sins and passions. Demons are cast out in the name of the Lord. In the name of God the Lord himself is omnipresent.

The elder instructed us frequently to pray constantly, without which it is very hard to possess the Holy Spirit.

'Acquire the habit of never beginning any business without prayer. If you are working at your trade, before anything else receive the blessing of the Queen of Heaven. Recite the Jesus Prayer before her face. Sense the presence of the Lord in your heart while you are working. He sees everything, even your thoughts and feelings. Try to unite with prayer your every

hand-copied extracts can be as spiritually valuable as they were in the Middle Ages. (Translator's note.)

movement, your every contact with an object. Prayer gives birth to humility, and without humility there is no salvation. When you finish work, offer up your thanks to the Lord and to the Queen of Heaven.

'My children, every time you go up or down stairs, say (to yourself) on every step a little word of your constant prayer. I do not give you my consent to go up or down stairs any other way.

'Do not say your prayers hurriedly. Prayer is both healthy for the soul and useful for the heart. "Let us not beat the air in vain."

'Every holy word is a creative power. Every word of a prayer draws us near to God. We have ruined our words by tearing them away from the Lord. Even if we need to say something worldly, we must keep a prayer in our hearts. If someone is not accustomed to keeping a prayer in his heart during a conversation, let him at least remember that he is speaking in the presence of God, and that he, our Father in Heaven who is present here, sees all that he is saying and feeling. One must never forget the omnipresence of God. To forget this is sin.

'A person who wants to establish constant prayer in his heart should not say anything superfluous or vain, and also he should not dream, worry, nor thoughtlessly do anything he fancies, but in everything try to do the will of God. Talk with the Lord as much as possible, my children, in your private prayers. This purifies the heart, strengthens the mind and gives power in actions to fulfil the will of God.

'When you say the morning and evening prayers, do not forget that prayer is conversation with God.

'So you have addressed God with the gracious words of the saints, and perhaps that is all you will do. It should not be all.

'After saying the prayers with great attention, one should stand at least for a few minutes with thoughts and feelings quietened, awaiting in one's heart understanding or an answer. These few minutes will teach you much: first three minutes, then five, and then you will see yourself how much each person needs. I ask you to carry this out and give you my consent for it. This will intensify your constant prayer and your renunciation of your own will, and will give you a thirst to receive (possess) the Holy Spirit in your heart.

'Prayer is the beginning of eternal life, it is a door through which we enter the Kingdom of Heaven, it is a road which leads us to the Lord and unites us with him. Without prayer a man does not live, but is continually dying, even though he does not realise it.

'My children, try to acquire a spirit of constant prayer. Beg it earnestly from the Mother of God who prays for us without sleeping, as I have already told you more than once.

'Be courageous even when the Lord sends great trials upon you.

'Passions overpower one, prayer weakens, and one does not even want to pray: all one's attention is swallowed up by different desires and passions. It is just here, as if on purpose, that such inward and outward misfortunes are encountered which will cause a weak man to fall into depression.

'This passion, depression, kills everything holy, everything living and human.

'You will sooner be crucified on the cross when you pray as many of our spiritual heroes used to pray in ancient times, struggling with their passions. Read "Let God arise and let his enemies be scattered."* If anyone has it, read the canon to the Honoured and Life-giving Cross of Christ, and then you will again be crucified on a cross and beg the Consoler of our souls and bodies to mollify you, to forgive you and to enter into your soul and drive out the terrible depression which is breaking you.

'Here are a few words from the canon to the Holy, Life-giving Cross:

'"O Cross, the resurrection of all, O Cross, the corrector of the fallen, the mortifier of passions, O Cross, the opposer of our designs. O Cross, you will be my strength, my stronghold and my power, the Deliverer and Protector against them who wrestle with me, my Shield and Defender, my Victory and my Confirmer, everlastingly watching me and protecting me.

'"Stretch out your hands, Blessed Maiden, Mother of God, in the form of a cross, in him who was raised up on a cross, and

* Psalm 67.2. (Psalm 68.1 in the English Bible).

bear today, O Virgin, the prayers of all those who pray faith-fully to you.'''

The elder Zachariah sometimes drove out evil spirits from pos-sessed people in our presence, praying first of all as though cru-cified on a cross.

It is impossible to describe all the miracles and all the admonitions of the elder Zachariah, since there were so many of them.

Not long before his death, Father Zosima journeyed to Sarov on a pilgrimage. Once he went to the Saint's stream, into which travellers used to plunge to be healed. He came up to it but could not make up his mind to enter the water. Finally, he sighed and said: 'Father Seraphim, you know that I am old, weak, ill and sickly, that I cannot endure cold water. How am I to bathe? I shall fall ill, and I won't make it home. Help me; heat the water.'

When the elder went into the water, it became very warm, almost hot. The elder remembered this with great gratitude.

Despite his dangerous illnesses, Father Zosima was always cheerful and thanked God for everything.

The spirit of constant prayer radiated in all his words and movements. He especially taught us to beware of depression. Depression is the threshold of hell, it kills will, feeling and reason.

The elder also often repeated to us the words: 'As I find, so shall I judge.' He told us this so that we should never forget the hour of our death, for at any moment we may be banished to eternity, and therefore we must always be preparing for it.

The elder greatly disliked talkativeness and said more than once: 'In paradise there are many repentant sinners, but not a single chatterbox.'

When the elder grew very weak and could not look after him-self, one of his spiritual daughters, Agrippina – or Grushatka, as he called her – began to help him every day.

She had spent all her youth in a monastery, living with her aunt, who was a nun. She had taken monastic vows there. After her aunt's death, Agrippina lived in the world, as a servant. She had little education and little spiritual experience, but she had a strong, monastic spirit.

When she came to the elder, she worked the whole time: mended linen, cooked, tidied everywhere, did the shopping, and so on. We called her the cell-maid. She was a good person, with skilful fingers, but rather stubborn and stern.

Once the spiritual daughter who wrote the elder's biography arrived at his dwelling. The elder said joyfully: 'At last, here is someone come to see me.' These words irritated his cell-maid. 'What are you saying, Father? Surely you don't mean that all of us sitting here are not someone?' But the elder had said this to test her humility. '"At last, here is someone come to see me," you said. But now I'll tell you something about her, and you won't call her someone, you won't be glad when she comes.'

And Grushatka began to tell him: 'Once on a feast-day I was in the Danilov Monastery. There was a crowd of people – but I saw your "someone" take Communion in the main part of the church, while I had gone off to the side chapel. I saw her come in and go here and there taking Communion; she took Communion in the main part of the church and at the side chapels on the right and the left. That's the sort she is.'

'Why do you say such improbable things, Grushatka? What's wrong with you? Surely you realise you're making up stories about me?' said the accused woman, looking at the elder and expecting him to make some remark to Grushatka. But the elder said nothing. Finally Grushatka went off to the kitchen, and the elder spoke up: 'Well, what sort of a spiritual daughter are you to me? So you couldn't stand just a small wrongful accusation, and started to justify yourself? Grushatka is coming back from the kitchen now; bow down to her on your knees and beg forgiveness.' The accused woman immediately did as the elder had said.

The elder had a great concern for the souls entrusted to him by the Lord. He often used to tell us about St John Golden-Tongue (Chrysostom – Translator's note), giving us a glimpse of the ocean of his love for men. He pointed out how varied are the forms of Christian love, which depend on human feebleness, and what judgement we need to have in order to love every person with the love which will assist the salvation of his soul. In order to achieve this virtue of judgement, we must possess constant prayer.

'I believe,' Father Zosima would say, 'that by abiding constantly before the face of our Abbess, the Queen of Heaven, doing nothing, but receiving her blessing, you will receive constant prayer and that love for everyone which is pleasing to Our Lord Jesus Christ. May I also remind you that at the end of any business you have begun, you should not forget to thank the Ever Virgin Mary the Mother of God with all your heart.

'Christ is given to the soul by his Most Pure Mother. Pray diligently to the Most Pure Lady and you will be with her son. Remember these words,' the elder said.

The elder also asked us to read carefully the Life of St Isidora, who was humiliated and offended on all sides. Many even considered her mad, and openly mocked her. She bore this with great Christian humility, serving everyone and loving those who hated her. She achieved holiness; the Holy Spirit lived in her heart. News of her reached a certain great elder, who arrived from a distant hermitage, fell at her feet, begged for her saintly prayers and talked with her, as with a vessel of the Holy Spirit. There was no limit to the surprise of her sisters who had insulted her.

The elder Zosima (who was called Zachariah as a *skhimnik*), ordered everyone to read the Life of the blessed Isidora. He instructed them to try to imitate inwardly her meekness and humility, that is, not to make oneself out to be better than others; to desire neither praise, nor honour, nor even love for oneself, but to seek exclusively the glory of God and his Truth, serving God and one's neighbours, merging with the Holy Trinity in prayer, in the fear of God and in full repentance, thinking oneself worse and more sinful than everyone else.

One day, sitting in his cell, the elder glanced into his holy corner, where his icons were. One look horrified him. Before the icons stood a demon, with a repulsive, horrible head in the shape of a coconut. He was standing there and gabbling the Psalms of David very fast.

'What are you doing? Surely you're not praying?' asked the

elder.

'I? I am outraging prayer,' muttered the demon, and vanished.

The elder warned us not to pray anyhow, without even hearing the words of our prayers, while our hearts were steeped in unprayerful feelings, with our thoughts wandering as they chose.

Prayer is not a mechanical activity, but a confrontation with God, a conversation with him.

'Pray humbly, then, in the fear of God, in awe, so that your prayer does not turn out to be an outrage of prayer.'

CHAPTER 7

Death

Finally his painful experiences undermined the elder's already weak health. He had to go out into the fresh air, and from time to time we would visit him there.

How the elder loved nature! He loved it in three different ways; as angels, children and sages love it. When he walked through the forest with us, we felt the power of his prayers, forgetting about everything earthly. It was as though ranks of angels surrounded us. The elder said very little when he was in the midst of nature, but if he did say something, then it was with such child-like joy and simplicity that his earthly age disappeared.

Once we were walking in the forest, and the elder said: 'It would be good if we were to find some white mushrooms, but for some reason there is not one today. I will ask the Lord to send us immediately twelve mushrooms, according to the number of the apostles, with the biggest and finest white mushroom standing in the middle, so that this group may remind us of the Saviour with his disciples.'

We walked and walked, but there were still no mushrooms. The elder's face shone, and he was praying the whole time. Within half an hour, to our surprise, we came upon a remarkably beautiful arrangement of white mushrooms. In the middle was a large white mushroom of unusual size and beauty, and around it were twelve white, smaller mushrooms, also firm and good. The elder looked at them, smiled and said: 'Forgive us, Lord, that we made our request like children, but you mercifully gave us consolation even in this.'

Nature for the elder was a book of the holy revelations of God. When looking at the sky, or at a flower, the elder revealed to us, like a sage, the mystery of the love to us sinful people in the

Trinity of the One God.

One cannot describe everything about the elder; he gave us so much, by his life and his exhortations and his prayer.

Sometimes the elder would get up during the night, fill some empty bottles with water from the water-pipe, and, quiet as a mouse, so that no-one should hear or see him, begin to wash the floors in his cell after his visitors had left. Next morning Grushatka, arriving at the elder's cell, would fall upon him: 'What's this? You're ill, but you've obviously spent the whole night washing the floor. I could wash it better than you in a quarter of an hour.'

The elder looked sadly at his cell-maid and said humbly: 'You will not be able to wash the floor as I wash it. You see, I know who comes to see me and sometimes I read a lecture to some of them in my prayers, and I pray deeply, very deeply about others, cleaning up the dirt on the floor and asking the Lord to clean the dirt from their souls in the same way, so that Christ may be resurrected in them, that the temple of their souls might shine brighter than the sun with all the virtues. It is not easy for me to wash the floor, I bend down with pain and I wash with pain. May they also not fear difficulties, obliterating everything in themselves which is not pleasing to the Lord. I even weep over these souls, praying for them, and rub the floor with water mingled with my tears . . . If I sometimes find such prayer for them necessary, why do you descend on me? I weep over my own sins too, and prepare myself to pass into eternity.'

At last our elder took to his bed, for he had become so ill that there was no hope of his recovery. He prepared joyfully to pass into eternity, and it was announced to him that he would die in a few days' time. The elder read the prayer for the dying to himself and sang the Easter canon in a barely audible voice. Then he suddenly felt in his heart that Bishop Trifon needed him and that the Lord would prolong his life and grant him a respite.

'What is this? Why?' the elder sighed in prayer. 'Why does Bishop Trifon need me so much? I think I'll call him to me. Let him say himself what all this is about.'

And then the elder took his rosary, put it to his forehead, and, in the presence of the landlady of his flat, E.G.P., said: 'Let this rosary now be a telephone for me. Trifon, my friend, come to me at once. I was ready to die, but my heart says that you still need me. Come, and let me talk to you.'

The landlady, looking at the elder with mockery, said: 'Now why are you clowning and acting the fool? Calling your rosary a telephone – are you a child playing some kind of game? Who will hear you? Yes, and even if you really were calling Metropolitan Trifon to you, he wouldn't come.'

'I have called him, and we'll see what happens,' said the elder meekly.

Within half an hour there was a ring at the door. They opened it. Metropolitan Trifon's sub-deacon had arrived, in order to warn them that the Metropolitan was on his way to the elder, that he had already set out.

The landlady's surprise knew no bounds.

The elders' meeting was very moving. With tears in his eyes, Metropolitan Trifon prayed for the healing of Father Zosima, (who was called Zachariah as a *skhimnik*), speaking thus: 'I need you; may the Lord prolong your life, may you pass into the other world after me, so that you may pray for my soul when it is flying through the torments.'

'Arise, elder, arise and confess me,' said Metropolitan Trifon.

'I can't, my dear Bishop, I can't even raise my head from my pillow, I can't . . .'

'Arise, as a duty.'

The elder raised himself with difficulty, and, supported by Bishop Trifon, went up to the icons, confessed his dear guest, and lay down again. He had grown worse.

The Metropolitan, bursting into tears, begged the Ruler of the World, our Lord Jesus Christ, to heal the elder. Bishop Trifon's whole heart was united with the Lord, his prayer was burning and fervent. He prayed also to the Queen of Heaven and Earth, that she, the Most Pure Mother of God, would move her Son by her entreaties to grant a respite before the death of the elder Zosima, that by a miracle the elder might rise and grow strong enough to officiate at a church service together with him (the Metropolitan).

They said their farewells. The elder lay on his bed, as white as a corpse.

Bishop Trifon, deeply moved by the elder's devotion to duty and love, but also deeply disturbed by his serious illness, went from him to the Church of the Ascension, where he had to officiate.

At the end of the service, Bishop Trifon made a speech to the people: 'Brothers and sisters, I beg you to pray for the ailing elder Zosima. Not everyone here knows him, but I will tell you what sort of a person he is. In my youth I lived in Petersburg with the rank of an archimandrite, and I was in such a terrible state that I wanted to abandon my rank and begin a completely different life. However, it was suggested that I should make the acquaintance of a certain monk of the Holy Trinity Monastery of St Sergius, who had arrived in Petersburg to collect alms and was no ordinary man. He will not be without interest for you. I expressed my desire to become acquainted with him. And then, after a night spent in conversation with him, the next morning my thoughts and feelings had become quite different. And it's thanks to this elder that you see in front of you the old, feeble Metropolitan Trifon.'

After this, the whole congregation fell on their knees and the Metropolitan held a petitionary service for the health of the seriously ill elder Zosima (who was called Zachariah as a *skhimnik*).

O, how diligently and fervently the Bishop prayed.

'For he is my mentor,' he said, 'who gave you Metropolitan Trifon, for it was he who led my soul out of the mist of temptations and gave to it the light and power of love. Now he is lying on his death-bed, he has become a great elder, in whose heart live thousands of beggars and wretches. He is near death. In your hearts, bow your knees again and again in prayer for my benefactor, the gravely ill elder Zosima.'

This collective petitionary service accomplished a miracle. Within a few days the elder felt better; he began to recover. When he was told about the petitionary service for him in the Church of the Ascension, Father Zachariah, smiling weakly, said: 'Yes, I've already heard, I've heard of the miracle of that "candle-end" Trifon.'

The elder called Bishop Trifon "candle-end" because he knew that his earthly life would end soon, very soon.

When the Bishop fell fatally ill, the elder prayed for him with touching love. And when he passed away, the elder's special prayers for him intensified, and he ordered us, his spiritual children, to remember the Bishop and all his dead spiritual children and relations.

The elder sent me to Bishop Trifon's grave. There were no flowers on it. The Bishop had not given his consent for his grave to be decorated. Crowds of people with tears in their eyes surrounded his remains. The Bishop was buried in the German cemetery.

'My friend Bishop Trifon wanted me to live for another two years after his death. Well, let it be so, according to his holy prayers.'

And our dear elder remained with us on earth for two years more.

Grown very weak, entirely immersed in prayer, he directed people's souls, as before, to the Lord, leading them to repentance, which regenerated them through his holy prayers.

It was as though he bore our hearts in his hands, restraining us by his prayers and his life. He tried to make us love and remember the Holy Trinity more deeply and more strongly, and strive towards the possession of the Holy Spirit in our hearts.

One time several of us had gathered together, and the elder began to teach us: 'To start a fervent struggle with the passions and the sins engendered by them, we must fear God: *that is the beginning of wisdom.* The wise man is he who has taken possession of the Holy Spirit, attempting to fulfil all the commandments of Christ, fearing to offend the Saviour by sin. And if he is wise, he is also humble; the higher a man is in spiritual terms, the more he sees how great God is and how insignificant and helpless he, the man, is, how sinful he is in comparison with that towards which we should strive.

'The greatest of the saints, St John Golden-Tongue (Chrysostom), said in his prayer before Communion: "I believe,

Lord, and confess, that Thou art indeed the Christ, the Son of the Living God, *come into the world to save sinners, of which I am first.*"

'One of you once said to me: "If you don't sin, don't repent." My children, this is a bad thought, it can lead a man into sin. Very well, if he has sinned, let him at least repent of the sin he has committed. No, there is nothing worse than sin. Sin gave birth to the devil. Avoid sin, struggle with the help of the Queen of Heaven against all that is evil. And the nearer you are to the Lord, the more the eyes of humility will be opened within you and you will be in a state of profound and constant repentance. And by repeating the Jesus Prayer: "O Lord, Jesus Christ, Son of God, have mercy on me, a sinner", you will be still nearer to the Lord and he will give you heavenly love for everyone, even for your enemies.

'Sometimes people experience such misfortunes as when a man, instead of striving to unite himself with the Lord by humility, lapses into arrogance, into enticements, into fancies and condemnation of others, considering himself to be almost a saint, and some of them even imagine that they are saints . . . Such people the Lord allows, as a punishment and as a means of teaching them, to sink into some most severe and shameful sin, under the burden of which they begin to come round. It's as though they come to their senses. They repent, and sometimes reform completely. But by no means does this always happen. Very often they perish. God forbid that anyone should be in their place.

'Once again I beg you and instruct you; be afraid of lapsing into sin. Do not crucify the Saviour over and over again by sins. Receive consent from the Queen of Heaven for everything and the Lord will send you the first stage of grace: recognition of your sins.

'Heed your conscience, which is the voice of God, the voice of your Guardian Angel. You must not fail to be concerned about your conscience, for you could lose it, it could become burned up and powerless, and then it would not be the voice of God. As for how to take care of your conscience, you will learn that from my elder, Father Ambrose of Optina, from whom I received consent to become a monk and exhortations for my whole life. Read his biography, his letters, and there you will find his reasoning on the conscience.

'Father Ambrose was a great sage; he possessed the grace of the Holy Spirit. Wisdom without grace is folly. You will understand that very well when you try to live for God and in God. Remember the words of Father Ambrose: "Where there is simplicity, there are a hundred or so angels, but where there is wisdom, there is not one."

'Aim for simplicity, which is given only by perfect humility. This cannot be explained in a few words, you will understand it through experience alone. One can live in God and for God only in humility and simplicity. Aim in humility for simple, holy love, perfect love, embracing all men, all, in prayer. Show mercy to the powerless, the sick, the misunderstood, the wretched, those bogged down in sin – imitate your heavenly protectors, the saints. Try to possess heavenly joy, so that you can rejoice with the angels over the repentance of every man who has lost his way.

'And so, my children, take care of this great gift of God, your conscience; it unites you with heaven, it punishes your weak, sinful will with the holy, omnipotent will of God.

'My dear children, you must have *a clear conscience*. Pray about this also to the Queen of Heaven, and ask the elders of Optina for help, remembering to pray for their rest.

'My little children, learn humility from the saintly elder Macarius of Optina, who taught my elder Ambrose in such a way that he ordered that he should be buried in the shirt of Father Macarius, who had been his spiritual father.

'The elder Father Macarius was undoubtedly saintly. The Queen of Heaven herself told me this, unworthy and sinful man that I am, when she appeared to me in a waking vision as I was on my way to the elder Ambrose. I prayed at Father Macarius's grave according to her instruction, as I have already told you.

'I beg you always to remember him. When we remember righteous men, then they also remember us at the throne of the Lord.

'So learn from Macarius of Optina, master everything which

he wrote to his spiritual children. There are three or four
volumes of letters which he wrote. I know of no better teacher of
humility for us. Lay up all his advice in your heart and put it
into practice. "Without humility there is no salvation." God
opposes the proud and gives grace to the humble. Always bear
in your hearts the Saviour's words: ". . . learn of me; for I am
meek and lowly in heart: and ye shall find rest unto your souls"
(Matt. 11.29).'

The elder sighed deeply and said: 'I am tired, my children, I
shall go and lie down now. You go home, and may the Lord and
the Queen of Heaven bless you. We shall see each other again
here; come to see me. Why are you looking at me so sadly? I
shall stay for a while longer on earth, and do not forget my
words.'

The elder seemed to melt away, he grew weaker and weaker,
but he still received all who came to him with great love and a
kind of intuitive attentiveness, consoling, encouraging and
teaching them.

The spiritual daughter of proto-priest Vladimir Bogdanov
came to him, weeping bitterly, and began to complain to him:
'My spiritual father has died, now I have no spiritual father and
I am left all alone, abandoned, no-one needs me. Father Vladimir, to whom I went for consolation, is no more.'

The elder interrupted her abruptly, with pain in his heart:
'How is he no more? He is now much more alive than when he
lived a temporary life on earth and was preparing to be translated into eternal life. If he is now standing at the throne of God,
he can see the Most Holy Trinity with his whole being, he can
see the Protectress of the Christian race, he is in communion
with the angels and the saints, so how is he no more? How dare
you tell such a lie, such an untruth? Now, when he can see the
souls of his spiritual children in all their depth, and knows them
incomparably better than when he was on earth, because he is
talking about them with their guardian angels and their heavenly protectors, and is ready to help his spiritual children together with them, if they turn to him . . . But you say that he is
no more, that you are alone – alone, how can that be? Or do you
want to forget him? To go away from him? Or else you have

forgotten that on the Day of Judgement he will say: "Here am I and my children"? Or perhaps, although you confessed to him, you were not his spiritual daughter, that is, your soul was not born again to eternal life through his prayers and advice and the duties and commandments that he imposed on you. Perhaps he did not exist for you when you saw him on earth and he spoke to you, taught you, absolved you from your sins and gave you Christ's Holy Sacrament? Perhaps you had a passion for him, you became accustomed to it, and so on . . . Tell me. Think everything over carefully and tell me.'

The visitor was silent, deep in thought. She sat for quite a long time in the elder's cell, looking at the icons, and it was obvious that something serious was taking place in her soul. The elder watched her affectionately, evidently praying for her. The visitor rose, went up to the elder, and said: 'Father, give me your blessing to come and talk to you tomorrow. My soul feels lighter, better . . .' 'Very well, my dear, come,' said the elder. Having received his blessing, she bowed and went out.

The elder's health grew worse and worse. His face became transparent, and he was like a shadow, so thin was he, but his eyes burned with the same divine fire of love to all the suffering, the sick, the lonely and the misunderstood.

Our elder took to his bed with cancer of the bladder and of his internal organs in general.

He lay there white as a sheet, with meek submissiveness, forgetting himself for the sake of others, completely immersed in prayer.

With his consent, I prepared for Communion by fasting with different spiritual fathers, and grew especially fond of one of them, an archimandrite from the Danilov Monastery, who had a great gift of love for human souls, and was overloaded with numerous people to confess, for whom he had such a concern that many of them even came to him to reveal their thoughts.

Becoming incredibly tired in church, because it was impossible to count all the people coming to confess, or to give his attention to each of them, he would go away to his cell, carrying off with him exercise books and sheets of paper, often covered with impossible, indecipherable handwriting – these revealed the thoughts of his spiritual children. And to each of them he gave a written reply to all their questions and perplexities, and made various extracts from the books of the Holy Fathers for their edification, separate extracts for each person, according to what he needed. Moreover, he made extracts from the Holy Fathers and the Spiritual Leaders of Piety for all his spiritual children in general. From time to time he fell ill. A very angel would have grown tired of such a burden, but a man, made of flesh . . .

I felt infinitely sorry for him, because I realised how much he loved and how much he endured, and how demons of different kinds would attack him, feeling malice towards his unearthly love for his spiritual children, and his concern for the salvation of their souls.

And so I went to our own dear elder, Father Zachariah. I knelt down beside his bed and begged him to pray for archimandrite Simeon and give him his elder's blessing, so that he might be able to cope with his spiritual children, no matter what the difficulties and temptations, and that the elder would obtain for him by prayer such strength that he would not fall ill, that the Queen of Heaven might help him in everything.

The elder took my request seriously. He remembered Father Simeon well in his prayers. He prayed for him and gave him his elder's blessing. Moreover, he sent an icon to him via me – a sign of his blessing. I handed it to Father Simeon. He was pleased, and said: 'The elder has passed part of his power on to me.'

The elder gave no more such blessings to any spiritual person.

Father Simeon, having learned from me that the elder was near death, and that he had imposed many commandments and instructions on me, which no-one would be able to rescind after his death, took pity on my feebleness and said: 'Just you go to your elder, Father Zachariah, and ask him to withdraw at least some of the duties, commandments and instructions he has imposed on you, because you may not be able to cope with them.'

I obeyed Father Simeon. I went to the elder's cell, and made three bows to the icons, as he had ordered us always to do when we went into a house where there were icons. I went up to the elder, and received his blessing. He told me to sit on a chair by his bed. At once he abruptly began speaking: 'My child, I beg you, I implore you, not to give up even one of the blessings and instructions which I have given you. It is not I who have laid them on you, but the Lord. Such is his holy will for you. May the Queen of Heaven give you her blessing to fulfil them all.'

I was struck by his intuition, and after what he had said, of course, I did not say a word about the purpose of my visit. Everything was settled. Such was the will of God, and the Queen of Heaven, despite my total feebleness and worthlessness, would help me to fulfil what had been laid on me, for the sake of the prayers of our elder the archimandrite-*skhimnik* Zachariah.

Things were very hard and difficult for the sick elder, and he had no peace at all, even during his fatal illness. Several times people came to him from the NKVD,* wishing to arrest him, but seeing that he was close to death they left him at home and put him under house arrest, so that he would not dare to receive people there.

We, his spiritual children, managed to force our way through to him very seldom at that time. The landlords were afraid to let us in, and besides there were many, many reasons which caused deep pain to his saintly heart, which loved all men, all . . .

Somehow I was lucky enough to get to the elder. He said to me: 'Already I remember you in prayer not as Elizabeth, but as the novice Elizabeth,' as though he were emphasising by this that I must become a novice and fulfil everything that had been laid on me.

I asked for his consent to go down to Poltava for a short while, to accompany there a sick person who was in great distress. The elder consented, for he particularly loved acts of charity, and the commandment of love had blended together with his heart. He seemed to peep into my soul as he gave me his consent, to say something wordlessly. I bowed and left. I left, but my heart

* The People's Commissariat for Internal Affairs, one of the antecedents of the present-day KGB. (Translator's note.)

was wrung with pain . . . but then, I was not going away for long. I would see my beloved father again, my dear elder, and then they were not allowing anyone into him now . . . For some reason I was choking with tears . . .

So there I was in Poltava. My sick friend was very pleased, but I felt wretched and not quite myself. I held out, and waited for letters from Moscow.

At last there was a letter from L.M. She informed me that our dear archimandrite-*skhimnik* Zachariah had died and been buried.

When I read this, I was seized by incredible grief, not because he had passed on into eternal life, where it would be much better for him than it had been on earth, but because I had gone away and had not seen his last moments on earth, had not been with his spiritual children by his body in his cell, had not been in church at his funeral, had not given him a last kiss, had not said farewell to him, had not been at his burial, had not been in the cemetery and had not prayed with him when his body, lying in the coffin, had been lowered into the grave.

I was unspeakably sad. I went off by myself, and wept bitterly as I read the Psalter. I went away and did not bid you farewell, my unforgettable, dear, beloved father . . . Suddenly I saw a door opening and Father Zachariah entered in his short monk's cloak with a cross and his priest's stole and came straight towards me. His eyes were so full of love and life that I forgot all my grief in an instant for sheer joy. I looked at him with Easter joy and my heart was filled with tenderness. Coming close up to me, he said: 'Now what's this, why are you sad? Don't be depressed, you know how I feel about depression. Let me absolve your sins.' He covered my head with his stole and absolved my sins. Then he looked into my eyes, with the affection and authority with which a mother looks at her baby, and said: 'You were so sorrowful because you had not said farewell to me, but there was no need at all for us to say farewell, because I am always with you.' And he vanished.

That is how my 'beloved father', as I always called him, consoled me.

When I arrived in Moscow, I set off to Grushatka (the elder's cell-maid) to find out all the details of the elder's death and burial.

The elder died in full possession of his faculties on 2 July according to the old style, 15 July according to the new style, 1936, about 10 o'clock in the morning, having committed all his spiritual children to the Queen of Heaven.

He had asked for his funeral to be held in the Greek Church, but the landlords were afraid to take him there. His body was taken to the Church of the Renowned Resurrection in Bryussovsky Lane for the funeral. Our long-suffering elder, the archimandrite-*skhimnik* Zachariah was brought in in his *skhimnik*'s attire and the coffin was set down in the main part of the church before the royal gates.

Shortly before the beginning of the service, the priest on duty, Father Nicholas Pospielov, came up to the coffin, turned to the people who had gathered there, and asked: 'Who ordained the archimandrite as a *skhimnik*? Perhaps it was not a hierarch of our church?'

No-one spoke. 'Well, I shall not say a burial service for him as an archimandrite.' He sat the elder up in the coffin, raised his body, removed the *skhimnik*'s attire from it and threw it out of the window.

All his children were inwardly stupefied, but kept silent – they realised that they must keep silent.

When Father Nicholas removed the *skhimnik*'s insignia from the elder's body, his hands were trembling violently. Soon after this he died.

After the funeral the elder's body was taken to the German cemetery. His spiritual daughter, God's servant Natalya, reverently carried the *skhimnik*'s attire which had been removed from him in church. Before the coffin was lowered into the ground, the elder's spiritual children arrayed him in his *skhimnik*'s attire. It was painful for all those who knew and loved him. But what was to be done?

As they were carrying the coffin to the grave, they found on the road a small icon of St Seraphim of Sarov, the Miracle-Worker. They hung the icon up. It was as though St Seraphim himself was present in this icon, watching as the elder was dressed again in the *skhimnik*'s attire which had been removed in the church, and accompanying with his prayer the body of the long-suffering archimandrite-*skhimnik* Zachariah as it was lowered into the ground. He had loved the Queen of Heaven as deeply as the Saint himself, who had left to his children the final instruction to fulfil the Rule of the Mother of God.

That was how some of the spiritual children of the elder Father Zachariah interpreted the icon of St Seraphim which they found.

CHAPTER 8

Signs and Wonders

When I heard all this, I felt a great desire to go and pray alone at the elder's grave. I went to the cemetery late on purpose, so that no-one would be there. I stood there weeping for a long time, till the stars came out in the sky. It grew dark. Time to go home. I knelt down, kissed the earth on his mound, and then suddenly I heard his voice, not with my ears, but with my heart: 'Don't go home now, but make your way to Grushatka.' 'O gracious, what is this? To Grushatka? The stars are already in the sky, and I am so tired . . . And perhaps Grushatka has already gone to bed, she goes to bed early – well then, how can I go to her? I'm in the German cemetery now, but Grushatka lives in Trumpet Square. You know how far away that is! I won't go, and that's all there is to it. Perhaps I just thought I heard the elder's voice. He taught us himself not to believe our own hearts. Perhaps this is something to do with the enemy. I won't go, and that's the end of it . . .'

Suddenly I heard Father Zachariah's voice a second time: 'Go, I instruct you. You will find everyone there, so go, don't delay.'

That meant that I had to go, if the elder instructed me. I remember the elder's attitude to his instructions. 'But why are you sending me so late?' And again I heard the elder's voice: 'Don't meditate, don't waste time. You will find one of my spiritual daughters there, who will dictate to you several incidents from my biography, which you need to note down, because you don't know them. Go on then, I instruct you, hurry up, go.'

Without delay I bowed to the elder's grave and set off to Grushatka in Tsvetnoi Boulevard on Trumpet Square, not daring to think anything further, only praying. I arrived – and what did I find? Grushatka had guests, drinking tea. They were celebrating the name-day of a close acquaintance of Grushatka's, Paraskeva. One of the ladies sitting at the table stood up, kissed me and said: 'Oh, what a good thing that you have come, I need you so much. Surely you know me? We met at the elder's, didn't we?' I remembered her, but had forgotten her name. 'I am Catherine Andreevna Visconti. The elder told me that you are writing his biography. I have seen so many of his miracles, he has told me so much . . . I have not forgotten one little word of his, I have a very good memory. My whole life has changed, thanks to the elder. I beg you earnestly to come to me and I will dictate all this to you. I live close by.' And she gave me her address. I was startled, and emotion towards the elder gripped my soul.

I visited Catherine Andreevna Visconti several times. She received me simply, cordially and affectionately.

When I went to her the first time, she asked me immediately if I had been to the elder's grave. I told her what had happened to me the last time I had visited his grave, and why I had arrived so late at Grushatka's, fulfilling his instruction which had been so unexpected for me.

'Yes, he was a great elder,' said Catherine Andreevna. 'You know, when I still knew nothing of his existence, and was not yet Orthodox, I had a dream: it was as though people were crowding inside my plot in the German cemetery. What was it? Why had they gathered there? I looked, and some elder was standing in my plot, a *skhimnik*, and people kept reaching out to him with entreaties, with requests, stretching out thin, emaciated hands.

'And what next, within a short while I became acquainted with the elder, the archimandrite-*skhimnik* Zachariah. After his death his body was buried in my plot. And up to this day sick and suffering people come to his grave and turn to him with entreaties, and the elder helps them according to their faith.

'Well, now let me dictate to you.

'I was not Orthodox, but I believed in God. Living in Moscow, I would go into Orthodox churches from time to time. And so one day, being sorrowful, I talked to a priest I knew from the church of St Nicholas the Bell-ringer, Father Alexander. I talked to him, and he suggested that I should get to know a certain great elder, who was called Zosima, or Zachariah as a *skhimnik*, a monk from the Holy Trinity Monastery of St Sergius, now an archimandrite. For myself, I had not the slightest desire to meet him, I was not Orthodox. As I have already told you, I was a believer, but I had not delved deeply into the faith and had no understanding at all of denominations.

'At this time a great misfortune occurred to one of my friends, a religious and unusually good person. I felt very sorry for her. I could not rely on my own prayers and decided, well then, I'll go to the elder, as Father Alexander advised, he can help her, if he's so great.

'I arrived and was admitted to a large room, where I saw that wonderful elder for the first time, dressed in a white overall. Without asking for any blessing, I said: "Hello", but he did not reply. I began to have misgivings. Then in a trembling voice I said: "Father, forgive me for disturbing you. I have a friend who is in great sorrow, pray for her." I made my way to a chair and sat down, and on the other side of the table the elder came up to his chair. Again he made no reply.

'This confused me and in a shaking voice I began to expound how good my friend was, how kind, and how unhappy. Finally my nerves gave way and I fell onto the chair and broke into sobs, and then for the first time I heard his voice: "Why are you covering someone else's roof when your own is bare?" To which I replied: "I have a roof, I am not without a room." "No, you have no roof, and why do you have icons of St Nicholas and of Our Lady the Mother of God, when in your church you are supposed to rely on the Crucifixion alone?" I was inwardly astonished, wondering how he knew all this, when he had never been in my house. "Father, you see, I love them very much and I always prostrate myself before St Nicholas the Miracle-Worker when I have any grief or sorrow, or simply sadness." "Oh, you love them, do you? Well, tell me please, I will pray for you now, but if you die, who will offer bread on your behalf at the Eucharist?* Do you have a cross?" "Yes." "Then who was it

* During the preparation of the Eucharist, the priest cuts small pieces of

who put it on you?" "I did." The Father laughed and repeated my reply: "I did."

'Then he turned to the icons and raised his hand. I was struck by the change in his expression. It became like something unearthly, divine, and he spoke quietly, pointing to the icons with his hand: "Should anything happen, I would fervently pray for her, for whom you keep beseeching me." After this I got up, bowed and said: "All the best to you, Father," and left.

'When I arrived home, I went up to my icon-case and in deep sorrow said: "So this is what I have come to, I have left one shore and not reached the other." An abnormal anxiety and trembling gripped me, and I was fretful. The elder's words: "Should anything happen," kept resounding in my ears. I ran to the priest who had directed me to the elder. I went into him with the words: "Father, I can't bear it any longer, I want to adopt Orthodoxy," and I told him about my visit to the elder.

'The day before I adopted Orthodoxy, I decided to seek out the elder and receive his consent to be converted. Not finding him at home, I went to the people with whom he was staying. I found the elder sitting in a small room, and he met me with unusual cordiality.

'"Father, I have come to ask for your blessing to adopt Orthodoxy." "I am very, very glad," was his reply. "I have just been telling off a possessed man, and the demon shouted so loudly, as he went into the cupboard" – and the elder began to pull at his ear – "that he almost deafened me. In talking to the demons, I asked them: 'Can you look at the cross?' 'No, we cannot, it is waiting for us.' 'And where is the dead arch-priest Ioann?' 'He was sentenced to four years for concealing sin.'"

'When the elder lectured the possessed, the demons cried out: "The elder Zosima is tormenting us, reading prayers of exorcism."

'The elder released many possessed people from the spirits that were tormenting them.

'After the conversation about demons I stood up, received his blessing and went towards the entrance.

bread out of the main loaf. He offers them up in the petitionary prayers, mentioning the name of a person for each piece of bread. (Translator's note.)

'The elder hurried after me and took my head in his two hands.

'Suddenly I noticed on his forehead delicate golden lines, like the brightly shining rays of the sun, issuing from his forehead and temples. I was startled, and at the same time my heart felt surprisingly light. Even walking down the street, I thought; can there be evil people in the world? It seemed to me that everyone was overflowing with the same joy as I. I sensed the grace given to me by the elder. Never had I felt such unearthly joy, rest and peace. This was the mercy of God, which I had received thanks to the elder's prayers.

'On the third day after I had adopted Orthodoxy, I went to the elder. I knocked at the door. He opened it himself, and exclaimed: "Ah, Catherine, show me your Orthodoxy!" "Father, I don't know how to show my Orthodoxy, but I have adopted it." "Well then, show your Orthodoxy." "On my honour, I don't know what to do." When he said to me insistently for the third time: "Show me your Orthodoxy", my gaze involuntarily fell on his icon-case, and I crossed myself. "There you are, now you're my sister, and we have One Mother."

'He came up to me, kissed me on the forehead and invited me to drink tea. Taking a small saucepan full of milk, he poured out all the cream into a glass for me, so that it filled the saucer too. Going up to the sideboard, he took three or four pounds of black bread and a large handful of sugar, about half a pound, and put it all beside my glass. Then I said to him: "Father, what are you doing? I can't eat all that." Without a word of a reply, he came up and blessed everything with the words: "Bringing before Thee thine of thine own." "Do you need bread?" he enquired. "Yes." Cutting a large slice, the Father blessed it and said: "This is my blessing to you, that you may never in your life want for bread. Do you have any white bread?" "No, Father." Then he gave me a piece of white bread, saying: "May there be white bread for you too."

'And then, because of the elder's prayers, a friend of mine living abroad, for whom I had formerly worked, remembered me and sent me three parcels from Riga, three parcels in a row. Each parcel consisted of 20 kilogrammes of white flour, 8 kilogrammes of sugar, 7 kilogrammes of rice, 20 tins of dried condensed milk, 2 kilogrammes of tea and 4 kilogrammes of cocoa. I had not written anything to her, it was because of the elder's prayers that she had remembered me and sent me such wonderful, rich parcels.

'Before receiving these parcels the following incident occurred. At that time I had no place to live, and I was hungry in those years. I was going to the elder when I met a beggar, and after much hesitation I gave him my last twenty-kopek piece. When I entered the elder's cell, and asked for his blessing, he immediately called me to his table: "Come here, come here." He pulled out the table-drawer, saying: "Take as much as you need, don't be ashamed, take it."

'Here is another wonderful incident, which teaches us not to believe all our dreams.

'A certain woman named Agrafena had a cow. She had a dream. St Seraphim appeared to her in the dream and told her to send milk to the elder Zosima. Without much thought, she poured out ten mugsful and asked her neighbour Stepanida to take the milk to the elder. Stepanida herself did not have the means of going to the elder, so she came to me and asked me to carry the milk to him in her place. This took place at Shrovetide. I gladly agreed. It was early morning. I arrived at the elder's and told him that St Seraphim, appearing to Agrafena in a dream, had ordered milk to be brought to him. The Father began from a distance repeatedly to make the sign of the cross over the wooden jug of milk, and, at length, pronounced: "St Seraphim cannot appear to such people as Agrafena. That was a demon. I will not accept milk from a demon."

'In Printers' Lane, on Trumpet Square, lived a certain widow, Anna Petrovna. Her sister fell down through carelessness and cracked her skull. They had to summon an ambulance. Her head was bandaged. The doctor said that she must have complete rest, but if vomiting began, there was nothing to be done – she would die.

'Anna Petrovna spent the whole night walking up and down the room and appealing: "My God, help us, Father Zosima, pray for us, pray, heal my sister . . ." Her sister began to vomit.

'In the morning there was a severe frost. As soon as he awoke, the elder immediately asked his cell-maid Grushatka, who had arrived early that day (she was also the servant of the elder's landlords), to call a cab-driver. "I am going out at once." "What are you thinking of, Father, in this frost! And just who is going to let you?" But the Father was implacable. When they arrived in Printers' Lane, Anna Petrovna opened the door, pale and worn out. "Father, I wasn't expecting you, why have you come out in such a frost? How glad I am." "You weren't expecting me?. . . Then why did you not give me any peace the whole night? Show me your patient quickly."

'Going up to the dying woman, he laid his hand on her head and prayed for a long time. A little while after this the sick woman, with her bandaged head, was drinking tea with them, and soon she went back to work.

'One woman, who loved her friend very much, learned that she was hopelessly ill and would have to have her leg amputated. She went to the elder, banged on his table with her fist, and said: "Pray for her, so that she may keep her leg and not go into hospital." The elder was not angry at her impulsiveness and said: "May it be done to you according to your faith." When she visited her friend a little while later, she was startled to learn that she had not gone into hospital, and that her leg was completely healed, to the astonishment of the doctors who were treating her.

'One day as the Father was officiating at a service in church, everyone was coming in and kissing the cross. One woman looked at it mockingly and did not approach. The Father went up to her and asked: "Why did you not kiss the cross?" She answered him with swear-words, abusing him as a priest and reviling everything sacred. The father stood and listened patiently. When she had nothing left to say, he asked: "Have you finished? And now I'll tell you something: I won't judge you because you have abused us, I won't judge you because, despite the fact that you're unmarried, you have a child. But how dare you not baptise him, when you yourself are baptised?" She went completely white and whispered: "How do you know all this?" Making no reply to this, the Father said: "I am sorry for you, you are perishing." He turned her around by the shoulders and said: "Get out." She began to sway, and slowly walked out. This had such an effect on her that she repented.

'I learned that the Father had fallen seriously ill, and I felt very sorry for him. I decided to go to him, and to pray for him. Moreover, it occurred to me that if I took an acathist to St Nicholas the Miracle-Worker and another prayer to the Saviour which I loved very much, and read them aloud to the elder, then he would be healed. I put the prayer and the acathist into my pocket and set off.

'When I arrived at the elder's, all my zeal faded. I was afraid to confess my intention. I went up to the elder, received his blessing and sat down humbly on a chair. But the elder at once asked me: "What have you got there in your pocket? Take it out and read it aloud to me in front of the icons." "It is an acathist to St Nicholas." "Well then, kneel down and read it." After I had read the acathist, the elder said: "Well, what else have you got in your pocket? Read it. Pray for me." I pulled out the prayer to the Saviour and read it.

'"Very good; now look and see that I am quite well, through your faith. Let us drink tea together." He got up from his bed hale and hearty and chatted to me, just as if he were not in such a serious situation.

'I saw many miracles the elder performed. I will dictate some of them to you.

'Towards the Great Feast of Easter I became so poor that I had positively not one kopek left. I wanted to receive the priest, and give him at least a small payment, but I had nothing. If I could obtain only three roubles I could get by somehow. No-one could lend me anything.

'I went with my sorrow to the elder, but did not have enough spirit to tell him about my poverty. Father asked me more than once: "What's wrong, then?" but I answered: "Nothing." With this I left him, but my heart had grown much lighter. When I returned home, I was told: "Some woman with her face completely covered came to see you and asked for this parcel to be given to you. We asked her who it was from, but she said it wasn't our business."

'I opened the parcel and found in it three roubles and a silk blouse. Because of the Father's prayers the Lord had sent me consolation and my desire to have three roubles was fulfilled. And the silk blouse fitted me exactly.

'One of the Father's spiritual daughters was warmly praising a certain unbelieving man. To this the elder said: "What sort of a good man is he, if he does not confess God? Take this onto your cross, that is, if you think he's good, accept the whole burden of his ignorance of God as your cross and try to do and say everything that will make him come to his senses and come to God, but by no means praise him."

'One day the elder was invited to the Golovinsky Monastery to officiate at a service of prayer for rain. The abbot of the Spaso-Peskovsky Monastery was officiating with him. During the prayers clouds began to appear, and, gradually thickening, were at length so low that the abbot said to Father Zosima: "Quickly, Father, or else the rain will fall at once." But the elder replied: "Don't hurry the service. When we finish everything the rain will fall, but it won't come yet." When they had performed the holy service for rain without haste, the Father went into the vestibule, raised his hand and said: "Right, you can come now." Immediately pelting rain poured down, soaking deep, deep into the earth.

'The elder Zosima always remembered in his prayers Metropolitan Philaret of Moscow, whom he deeply respected, and for whose saintly life he had great reverence.

'One day one of the elder's spiritual daughters fell seriously ill. The doctors said death was inevitable. The poor woman was dying. Her relatives begged the elder to visit her for the last time.

'The elder Zosima said a prayer, took up a portrait of Metropolitan Philaret, hid it and said: "It is not I who am going to this sick woman, but the Metropolitan himself who will go and heal the sufferer." He made ready and set off. The sick woman had a son who was considered not altogether normal. He was a peculiar sort of person, such as are customarily called simpletons in the world. As soon as the elder began to approach the house, the abnormal youth suddenly said to his mother:

"Mummy, Metropolitan Philaret is coming to us, Metropolitan Philaret himself." "What is this? You've gone quite mad, my poor boy," groaned his mother. A few minutes later the elder entered the entrance hall. The simpleton rushed to take his fur coat, saying: "Your Grace, Father, allow me to take your coat." The dying mother listened to her son's words with dread. But then the elder came into the room and said: "Receive a blessing, not from me, but from Metropolitan Philaret. He has come himself to heal you." He let her touch the prelate's portrait.

'"So that means my son was right when he said the Metropolitan was coming to visit us."

'"Yes, he was right; the Holy Spirit revealed the truth to him. Well, you get up now and make us all some tea."

'"How can I? Why, I can't even turn over!"

'"You couldn't, but now you're well," said the elder.

'To her surprise, the woman felt quite well, and she got up and began her housewife's tasks. Her relatives were amazed, but the elder said: "Why are you surprised? Surely you know that Metropolitan Philaret can perform miracles, and you have now become witnesses of one of his miracles. Your mother was close to death, but now she is more healthy than any of you. Glory to God in his Saints."

'The elder always remembered to pray for the repose of Metropolitan Philaret, and instructed his spiritual children always to remember this great preceptor of Orthodoxy.

'One day a priest came to the elder, very unhappy. He had lapsed into dreadful passions and had completely forgotten the aim of our earthly existence. His words and actions produced a repulsive impression.

'One of the elder's spiritual daughters would not receive his blessing. In the presence of this straying pastor the elder said sternly to her: "Catherine, even though he is Gavrila, a pig's snout, he possesses the grace of priesthood, so you must receive his blessing."

'In this way he unmasked the priest in front of all those who were present, and humbled his spiritual daughter, pointing out to her the great significance of the priestly blessing. The elder's unmasking was not in vain. The errant pastor repented deeply of trampling on the grace of the priesthood by his sins, and because of the elder's prayers and love he broke out of the net of sins and passions. It was as though he was born again.

'"There is One Lord Judge who knows everything and everyone. My children, do not sit on the Throne of the Judge and Creator, on the Throne of the God who knows the human heart. Never judge anyone. It's really terrible for me to think that any one of my spiritual children would ever dare to do so.

'"Again I say, if you envy anyone, then you judge the Lord himself, questioning why he has not given you the blessings with which he has endowed some of your neighbours. Do you realise what a great sin envy is? Remember once and for all: a man who harbours condemnation and envy will never receive the Holy Spirit in his heart.

'"A man who judges can never be in the slightest degree humble, and without humility there is no salvation."'

This is what Catherine Andreevna dictated to me.

CHAPTER 9

Father Zachariah's Spiritual Legacy

In his last months the elder lay in bed almost all the time. He spoke seldom, and if he did say anything, it was for the benefit of souls. 'Do not forget that the first commandment of the Gospel summons us to repentance: "Repent and believe in the Gospel. These are the words of the Lord Himself" (Mark 1.15).

'Acquire virtues, which oppose sins.

'Never be depressed on any occasion or under any circumstances. Depression is a hangman which kills the energy essential for the receiving of the Holy Spirit in one's heart. A depressed person loses the ability to pray and is dead as far as spiritual feats are concerned.'

The elder's illness was so terrible that anyone else would simply have shouted with pain and complained unceasingly, but the elder Zachariah suffered in silence, offering up thanks to God for everything he sent.

The elder's face became like a face painted on an icon. It was obvious that he was retreating entirely into deep and secret prayer.

He behaved with such motherly attention and love to those who came to him that it seemed as though his suffering body did not exist. His soul embraced everyone who turned to him with divine love, completely forgetting about himself.

One day the elder got up from his bed, barely able to stand, went up to the icons, and, with a kind of special reverence, crossed himself. Then, turning to us, he said: 'Make the sign of the cross over yourselves more often. Remember: when the cross is lifted up, the ranks of the spirits of the air will fall.

'O Lord, you have given us your cross as a weapon against the devil.

'To my regret, I have seen that some people simply wave

their hands about, without even touching their forehead and shoulders. This is pure mockery of the sign of the cross. Remember what St Seraphim said about making the sign of the cross correctly. Read his admonition on this.

'My children, this is how you should order your prayers, which are an appeal to the Most Holy Trinity. We say: "In the name of the Father" holding three fingers together, showing by this that the Lord is One in Three Persons. Touching the forehead with three fingers, we sanctify our mind, offering up a prayer to God the Father, the Almighty, the Creator of angels, of heaven, of earth, of men; the Creator of all that is visible and invisible. And then, touching the lower part of the breast with these fingers, we experience all the torments of the Saviour, who suffered for us, we live through the crucifixion of our Redeemer, the only-begotten Son, born of the Father, begotten not made. And we sanctify our heart and all our senses, raising them up to the earthly life for the Saviour, who for our sake and the sake of our salvation came down from heaven and was made man.

'Then, raising our fingers to our shoulders, we say: "And of the Holy Spirit." We ask the Third Person of the Most Holy Trinity not to desert us but to sanctify our will and graciously to help us; to direct all our strength, all our actions towards possessing the Holy Spirit in our hearts.

'Finally, humbly, reverently, with the fear of God and with hope, and with deep love for the Most Holy Trinity, we end this great prayer, saying: "Amen", that is, "So be it".

'This prayer is always united with the cross. Think this over.

'How many times I have felt with pain that many people say this prayer quite mechanically, as though it were not a prayer but something one should say before beginning to pray. Never do this. It is sin.

'No business on earth is more important than prayer – none. Prayer gives birth to the simple virtues. I could tell you a good deal, but I don't have the strength,' said the elder, scarcely able to reach his bed. When he lay down, he seemed to be already dead. One of us burst into tears.

Immediately, in a barely audible voice (it was obviously

difficult for him to speak), the elder said to console us: 'My children, after death I shall be much more alive than I am now, so don't grieve when I die, be afraid of excessive grief – it can lead us into depression. Only be sure to remember that your endeavour to possess the Holy Spirit, your love for the Saviour, Our Lord Jesus Christ, and your endeavour to fulfil all his commandments, your trembling, reverential bowing down before God the Father in awe and in the greatest humility, will fill my heart with joy, for after all I am your spiritual father. I instruct you to endeavour with all your strength to achieve this.'

In silence the elder blessed us all and shut his eyes. We bowed down to the ground to him and dispersed.

One day, when the elder could no longer get up from his bed, one of his spiritual daughters who had not seen him for a long time came to him. She grew sad when she saw that he was so seriously ill, but she did not realise that the elder was already close to death and began to ask that as soon as he felt better, he would come to see her. The elder smiled sadly and said: 'Don't grieve, I shall soon drive past your flat, so you just come out and see me home. 'Why Father, how shall I know when you drive past? Who will you send to me, so that I can come out, and why don't you yourself drop in?' 'You will sense it yourself, the Lord will bring it to pass.'

The woman stopped asking him to come, not daring to ask for any amplification. She got up, fearing to weary the elder by conversation, bowed, received his blessing and left.

One day she was washing the floor in her flat. Suddenly an unusual fragrance enveloped her, as though a mass of beautifully-scented flowers had been carried into her flat. 'What is this? I have never smelt such a wonderful smell. Goodness me, where is it coming from, what is it?' She went to the window and saw a funeral procession, and at once went out into the street and asked: 'Who is being buried?' Her heart was painfully wrung. 'This is our elder driving past my flat, as he told me; and he let me know about it by that wonderful smell.' And she set off to accompany him to his grave, remembering his words: 'And then you will come and see me home.'

Many more miracles were performed during the elder's life and after his death, but I will not write them down yet. I will write them as a supplement to the biography, with God's help. I must visit a few more people and write down all the miracles accurately. I must check those I know and then describe them, so that I can answer for the authenticity of what is written.

The elder often appeared in dreams to his spiritual children: some he warned against all kinds of dangers, to others he gave his blessing for various good deeds, and others again he forbade to put their intentions into practice.

In this way we, his children, still live under our elder's guidance.

On the fortieth day after Father Zosima's death, I was in the cell of archimandrite Simeon (called Daniel as a *skhimnik*) in the Danilov Monastery. Father Simeon had long known and revered the elder, and had entrusted his own soul to him. He said that it would be better for me to die than to disobey the elder Zachariah in any way. On that day Father Simeon wished to read the burial service over the elder again himself. What a moving burial service it was. Never will I be able to forget it.

After the burial service the seriously ill Father Simeon turned to the elder Zachariah in entreaty, asking him about what was most important for him.

Father Simeon had a deep love and trust for our dear elder Zachariah. He forbade me to call him 'my elder' – 'He is not only your elder, but mine too,' said Father Simeon.

Father Zachariah strove to inspire us with a deep love for the Most Holy Trinity and Orthodox worship of it in prayer and in life.

One of Father Zachariah's spiritual daughters asked that at the end of his biography should be added an extract from the conversations of proto-priest Rodion Putyatin, 'On the One God, glorified in the Trinity', because it is very helpful in understanding Christian teaching on the Holy Trinity.

Here is the extract:

'Brothers, why do we so often remember in our prayers the

Father, the Son and the Holy Spirit? We pray to them at every divine service, there is hardly a single prayer in which we do not make mention of them. Why is this? It is because the Father, the Son and the Holy Spirit are our God.

'Why do we not call God simply God, but the Father, the Son and the Holy Spirit? Jews and Mohammedans also believe simply in God, even in the One God, they do not know that God is the Father, the Son and the Holy Spirit; only we Christians know that, who worship the true God. And true Christian faith is distinguished from wrong, false faiths above all by this, that it teaches us to believe in the One God, the Father, the Son and the Holy Spirit.

'Why is it necessary to know this, that God is the Father, the Son and the Holy Spirit, that He is One in Three Persons?

'If we did not know that God is One, but in Three Persons, then we would not know how God loves us. We would not know that He gave us His Only-begotten Son to be our Redeemer, so that everyone who believes in Him might not perish, but have eternal life. We would not know that we have a Saviour, the Son of God, who came down from Heaven to be our Saviour, was made man, suffered, died on the cross, rose from the dead, ascended into Heaven and sat down at the right hand of God the Father; we would not know that we have a Holy Spirit, who lives and works in us, to be our Sanctifier, who edifies and purifies us. To put it briefly: if we did not know that God is One, but in Three Persons, we would not be Christians.

'The One God, who appeared on Mount Sinai and laid down through Moses the law: the Lord your God is One Lord – he is the same who revealed himself in Jordan in three persons.

'And what did Christ order His disciples to teach everyone, when He sent them out to preach? Just this, that they should believe in the Father, the Son and the Holy Spirit. Thus, the fact that God is Father, Son and Holy Spirit is a shortened form of Christian teaching, a concise symbol of our faith. Faith which does not teach belief in the Father, the Son and the Holy Spirit is not Christian faith, not faith from grace, not saving faith.

'Everyone believes in God in a general way to a greater or

lesser degree: there is not and never has been a people in the world who did not believe in some kind of divinity. Without faith it is impossible to be saved, impossible to please God. However, one may say to you, with your faith, that it is impossible not to be saved, if only you wish it, impossible not to please God. But you know, when you appeal to the Father and the Son and the Holy Spirit for your salvation, then God the Father turns to you with all His love, God the Son intercedes for you with all His merits and the Holy Spirit is at work within you with all His life-creating power.'

Another spiritual daughter of the archimandrite-*skhimnik* Father Zachariah asked that at the end of his biography should be added a certain church legend which she had heard from an elderly nun who lived near Alma-Ata, in the mountains. This nun knew elders who were *skhimniki*, praying for the whole world.

Probably one of them was her confessor, and related to her this most moving legend, with which the elders warmed their hearts, uniting them in the constant Jesus Prayer of penitence with God in the One Trinity.

Here is this church legend:

'Hanging on the cross, nailed to it, worn out, covered in blood, the Son of God, our Lord Jesus Christ, our Creator and Redeemer, suffered for the sake of our salvation and yielded up His spirit to His Heavenly Father. '''Father, into thy hands I commend my spirit.' And when He had said this, He gave up the ghost'' (Luke 23.46).

'''When the even was come, there came a rich man of Arimathaea, named Joseph; he went to Pilate, and begged the body of Jesus. Then Pilate commanded the body to be delivered'' (Matt. 27.57–58).

'''And there came also Nicodemus, which at the first came to Jesus by night, and brought a mixture of myrrh and aloes, about a hundred pound weight'' (John 19.39).

'Having received permission from Pilate to take the body of Jesus Christ down from the cross and bury Him, Joseph and Nikodim prayed at the cross, covered in tears, in the greatest reverence, emotion and fear of God: "O Lord, how are we to touch your Most Holy Body, what prayers are we to recite? Our hearts are overflowing with deepest love for you, with worship of you. But we do not dare to touch your body. Teach us with what words and with what prayer we are to take you down from the cross." When they looked at the Saviour's face, they both began to tremble.

'The lips of the dead Jesus Christ began to move, and He pronounced: "In the name of the Father and of the Son and of the Holy Spirit."'